Jenny Ridgway ... Ridgway

Healthy Eating

Recipes & Investigations

Oxford University Press 1989

Oxford University Press, Walton Street, Oxford OX2 6DP

Oxford   New York   Toronto
Delhi   Bombay   Calcutta   Madras   Karachi
Petaling Jaya   Singapore   Hong Kong   Tokyo
Nairobi   Dar es Salaam   Cape Town
Melbourne   Auckland

and associated companies in
Berlin   Ibadan

Oxford is a trade mark of Oxford University Press

© Jenny Ridgwell, Judy Ridgway 1989

ISBN 0 19 832757 9

Acknowledgements

Photos are by Chris Honeywell pp. 9, 10, 14, 36, 55 (both); Janet
MacKenzie p. 19 (inset); John Walmsley p. 19 (main).

Poster on p. 71 courtesy Fresh Fruit and Vegetable Bureau.

Cover and all recipe photos are by Steven Lee.

Illustrations are by Caroline Brunt, Sara Carpenter, Sian
Leetham.

Handwriting is by Elitta Fell.

Food preparation by Louise Pickford and Jenny Ridgwell.

Set by Tradespools Ltd, Frome, Somerset
Printed in Hong Kong

CONTENTS

Symbols

Q = questions

e = experiment

i = investigation

◆ = recipe which is high in fibre

◆ = recipe which is low in energy

◆ = recipe which is a good source of protein

✎ = amount per serving

❧ = % of recommended daily amount

PREFACE

Recipe choice

This book aims to introduce students to a wide variety of new and different foods from many cultures. We think the recipes are healthy and delicious – a good start down the road to health. Most recipes can be prepared and cooked within one hour, an important factor in many schools where lessons are short. Special emphasis has been put on recipes which require little cooking or no cooking at all. We have also deliberately included several recipes where students can invent their own versions. Since healthy eating should be enjoyable, we have included sweet as well as savoury recipes, and special treats such as Chocolate Truffles.

The choice of ingredients

Healthy eating is a matter of balance – eating a variety of foods that you enjoy, including fruits, vegetables, meat, fish, dairy foods, and cereal foods. The balance also means not eating too much fatty or sugary food. Consequently we have used a wide variety of ingredients in the recipes. We feel that healthy eating is not a matter of simply substituting wholemeal flour for white flour or polyunsaturated margarine for butter. Indeed some dishes taste even nicer if they are made with white flour or butter. Provided these foods are not eaten very often, they can still form part of a nutritious and healthy diet.

How are the recipe sections organized?

The sections have been divided, for convenience, into important food groups such as roots and bulbs, cereals, and fruit. Meat, fish, and dairy products are used throughout the book and find their natural place within the various recipe sections. Separate sections for these foods were not thought necessary, as we did not wish to emphasize them as being 'good' or 'bad' foods.

Investigative and written work

GCSE guidelines encourage students to investigate, evaluate, and make decisions for themselves. Throughout the book, practical investigations, food tables, and data have been introduced and work set around them. In the introduction we concentrate on factors which contribute to a healthy diet, and investigations and written work are linked to this theme. Not all terminology is explained. For example, the phrase 'protein in the diet' is left unqualified, since other books adequately supply this information.

Practical investigations in each section are deliberately linked to the ingredients in recipes, so these investigations can be undertaken as an introduction to or an extension of the cooking session. Throughout the book, charts and food tables are introduced, and students are encouraged to compare nutritive values and extract information from data.

Nutritive calculations and RDAs

For calculations for the percentage of the recommended daily amounts of nutrients (% RDA), the following daily requirement of dietary energy and nutrients has been taken:

dietary energy 2150 kcal, 9000 kJ
protein 53 g
fat 83 g
dietary fibre 30 g
calcium 700 mg
iron 12 mg
vitamin C 25 mg.

> Note:
> $1 \, kcal = 4.2 \, kJ$
> (approx)

These figures are based on the nutritional requirements of a 12–14 year old girl, using data from *Food Tables* by Bender and Bender. However, students wishing to find their own nutritional requirements should use the charts on page 6.

Food tables do not usually provide a figure for the recommended daily amount of fat which should be eaten. However, for the purposes of comparing the fat content of recipes, this figure was considered important. The COMA report of 1984 studied the relationship between diet and cardiovascular disease. The report recommended that the total fat eaten should provide 35% of dietary energy. The 83 g recommended in the table represents 35% of the dietary energy requirements of a 12–14 year old girl (total energy requirements 2150 kcal, 9000 kJ). Other groups can work out their RDA for fat based upon energy requirements for their group.

At the end of each recipe, the percentage contribution which that recipe makes to the recommended daily amount of nutrients is shown. Figures for the calculation of nutritional values of food vary according to the source used. Foods themselves vary in their nutritional content, so for example no two 100 g portions of minced beef are exactly the same. Where possible, *Food Tables* by Bender and Bender has been used. Where data is not available, then a similar food value for a food has been substituted. So for 'raw spinach', where the figures are not available, 'watercress' has been substituted in the calculation. Calculations have been approximated to simplify the text. The % RDA is based on these original figures and so may not correspond exactly with the calculation. All attempts at accuracy have been taken, but the authors would be grateful if any errors are brought to their attention.

For some GCSE investigations and A-level work, students might need to calculate the % RDA of their own recipes. There are also several computer programmes available which show how foods and dishes provide a proportion of the RDA. The technique for this calculation has therefore been explained on page 7.

INTRODUCTION

What is meant by a healthy diet?

The food that we eat or drink is called our **diet**. So a healthy diet means eating the right kinds of food and drink to keep us in good health. All food provides us with **nutrients**, which are the parts of food essential to keep us healthy and alive. Nutrients help us to grow, keep our bodies in good repair, and help us stay fit and active. Foods which provide us with a variety of nutrients are called **nutritious foods**.

Dietary goals have been issued in the UK which suggest ways in which we can improve our eating habits. The NACNE report (National Advisory Committee on Nutrition) was issued in 1983, followed by the COMA report in 1984 on diet and heart disease. These reports recommended that we should:

- eat less fatty food, especially fats high in saturated fatty acids such as butter and lard
- cut down on the amount of sugar that we eat, from foods such as sweets and fizzy drinks
- eat more cereal foods such as bread and pasta
- increase the amount of dietary fibre eaten, found in cereals, fruits, and vegetables
- eat less salt – cut down on salty snacks, for example
- drink less alcohol – found in beer, spirits, and wine.

How can you adapt your favourite recipes to fit in with these healthy eating goals? Here are just a few tips. Add ideas of your own to this list:

- use polyunsaturated margarine and oil instead of butter, suet, and lard
- fry meat such as minced beef or bacon in its own fat – drain off any runny fat before completing the recipe
- choose fish or white meats such as chicken or turkey instead of red meats such as beef and lamb
- try using liver, kidney, and heart in cooking – they are good sources of iron and B vitamins
- use skimmed or semi-skimmed milk instead of whole milk
- cut down on the fat content supplied by cheese

by either using a smaller quantity of strongly flavoured cheese or a low fat cheese
- cut down on the sugar added to recipes
- choose fruit canned in its own juice or unsweetened fruit juice
- use more wholemeal flour and wholemeal pasta in recipes.

How much should we eat?

Health experts have worked out the amounts of different nutrients that we should eat each day. The amount of food that we need varies according to our age, size, sex, and the sort of work we do. For this book the authors have chosen the **recommended daily amounts of nutrients** (**RDA** for short) for a 12–14 year old girl. These are:

dietary energy 2150 kcal, 9000 kJ
protein 53 g   calcium 700 mg
fat 83 g   iron 12 mg
dietary fibre 30 g   vitamin C 25 mg

If you want to work out your own food needs, then check the charts on page 6. These charts are also useful if you need to work out other people's particular food needs, for example those of a pregnant woman or a young child.

What do the tables at the bottom of the recipes mean?

For each recipe, two figures are given. The first (marked ♪) is the number of kilocalories/ kilojoules or the number of grams of protein, fat, and fibre included in one serving of the recipe. The second (marked ✖) is the percentage of the recommended daily amounts of nutrients which one serving would provide. This is a complicated bit of maths, needing the help of a calculator! For those of you curious to know how it is done, here is the method. (You may also have to work out the % RDA for your own recipes at a later stage.)

Recommended Daily Amounts of nutrients

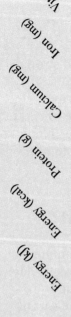

Boys	Energy (kJ)	Energy (kcal)	Protein (g)	Calcium (mg)	Iron (mg)	Vitamin C (mg)
under 1 year	—	—	—	600	6	20
1 year	5.0	1200	30	600	7	20
2 years	5.75	1400	35	600	7	20
3–4 years	6.5	1560	39	600	8	20
5–6 years	7.25	1740	43	600	10	20
7–8 years	8.25	1980	49	600	10	20
9–11 years	9.5	2280	57	700	12	25
12–14 years	11.0	2640	66	700	12	25
15–17 years	12.0	2880	72	600	12	30
Men 18–34 years						
sedentary	10.5	2500	63	500	10	30
moderately active	12.0	2900	72	500	10	30
very active	14.0	3350	84	500	10	30
Men 35–64 years						
sedentary	10.0	2400	60	500	10	30
moderately active	11.5	2750	69	500	10	30
very active	14.0	3350	84	500	10	30
Men 65–74 years	10	2400	60	500	10	30
Men over 75 years	9.0	2150	54	500	10	30

Girls	Energy (kJ)	Energy (kcal)	Protein (g)	Calcium (mg)	Iron (mg)	Vitamin C (mg)
under 1 year	—	—	—	600	6	20
1 year	4.5	1100	27	600	7	20
2 years	5.5	1300	32	600	7	20
3–4 years	6.25	1500	37	600	8	20
5–6 years	7.0	1680	42	600	10	20
7–8 years	8.0	1900	47	600	10	20
9–11 years	8.5	2050	51	700	12	25
12–14 years	9.0	2150	53	700	12	25
15–17 years	9.0	2150	53	600	12	30
Women 18–54 years						
most occupations	9.5	2150	54	500	12	30
very active	10.5	2500	62	500	12	30
pregnant	10.0	2400	60	1200	13	60
lactating	11.5	2750	69	1200	15	60
Women 55–74 years						
moderately active	8.0	1900	47	500	10	30
Women 75 years	7.0	1680	42	500	10	30

Source: Bender and Bender, Food Tables

Q What percentage of the RDA would a slice of chicken and carrot loaf provide?

The food value for one slice of chicken and carrot loaf:

k cal	kJ	protein	fat	fibre
150	620	10 g	9 g	2 g

The percentage of the RDA of **energy** can be worked out like this:

$$\% \text{ RDA energy} = \frac{\text{energy value of food} \times 100}{\text{RDA of energy}}$$

$$= \frac{150}{2150} \times 100 = \text{approx. } 7\%$$

The percentage of the RDA of **protein** can be worked out like this:

$$\% \text{ RDA protein} = \frac{\text{grams of protein in food} \times 100}{\text{RDA of protein}}$$

$$= \frac{10}{53} \times 100 = \text{approx. } 19\%$$

The percentage of the RDA of **fat** and **fibre** can be worked out in a similar way. Remember that the RDA of fat is 83 g and the RDA of fibre is 30 g.

How have the recipes been chosen?

If you eat a variety of different foods, your diet should contain all the nutrients you need to keep you healthy. So when we chose the recipes for this book, we decided to use as wide a variety of different fruits, vegetables, cereals, and seeds as possible. Each recipe can be quickly prepared within the normal Home Economics lesson, and we hope you will find the ideas attractive, delicious, and not expensive.

Since health experts recommend that we cut down on saturated fat, sugar, and salt, we have used polyunsaturated oil for most cooking, and cut down on the traditional amounts of these ingredients used in recipes. Other dietary guidelines have been followed such as using wholemeal flour, rice, and pasta, but sometimes you will find that recipes contain white flour and even butter! This is because in these recipes we thought the flavour and texture were better. And after all, you should enjoy eating!

Some of the recipes have been labelled with symbols, so that if you are looking for recipes to fit particular nutritional needs, you will be able to see at a glance which recipes will be most suitable.

- Recipes which are high in fibre; these will contain ingredients such as wholemeal flour, bread, beans, and peas. Fibre is important as part of a healthy diet.

- Recipes which are low in energy (i.e. provide few kilocalories or kilojoules): these are suitable for people who wish to lose weight.

- Recipes which are a good source of protein: these will contain meat, fish, cheese, eggs, or seeds such as beans and peas.

Where appropriate, dishes which are particularly rich in calcium, iron, vitamin C, or vitamin A have also been labelled.

What is the difference between a good and a rich source of a nutrient?

vitamin C in 100 g	
parsley	150 mg
orange juice	50 mg

Look at the food table showing the vitamin C content in 100 grams of parsley and of orange juice. Parsley is a *rich* source of vitamin C, but since 100 g of parsley could fill a bucket, it is not a *good* source. That amount of parsley would be difficult to eat. Orange juice, on the other hand, is a *good* source, because you could easily drink a glass (200 ml/200 g) which would provide 100 mg vitamin C – four times the amount you need each day.

Q Use food tables to find your own example of a rich and a good source of a nutrient.

Energy from food

Food is essential to provide us with energy. Our bodies need energy to move, for different parts of the body such as the heart and lungs to work, and to keep us warm. When food is eaten, it is broken down by the body. Some of the food is used as 'fuel' to be 'burnt up' by the body to give us energy.

e When food is burned in air, it releases energy in the form of heat. This experiment shows how this energy can be used to warm up a test tube of water. Try burning other foods such as crisps and cornflakes.

You need:

test tube
test tube holder
large unsalted, unroasted peanut
mounted needle or needle on a cork
thermometer

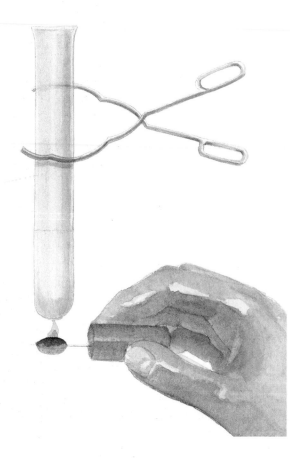

1 Put 20 ml of cold water in a test tube and measure the temperature.
2 Spear the peanut carefully onto the needle, then light the nut using a gas cooker ring or Bunsen flame.
3 As soon as it burns, hold it under the test tube of water, so that the flame heats up the water. If the nut goes out, relight at once.
4 After 1–3 minutes, the flame goes out, leaving a charred, black nut. Measure the temperature of the water and record the results on a chart.

temperature of water at start	temperature after heating etc.

Q 1 Write down what happened to the peanut, the test tube and the water during the investigation.
2 Why do you think the water heated up?
3 How was some of the heat from the peanut lost during your experiment?

How does fat fit into a healthy eating plan?

Health experts recommend that we cut down the amount of fat that we eat. We should eat more cereals and vegetables and less fried and fatty food. Most fats found in food contain saturated and polyunsaturated fats, but in different proportions. Health experts also suggest that we should eat foods which contain a higher proportion of polyunsaturated fat. Current research has found that a diet rich in fat, especially saturated fat, may lead to heart disease and overweight.

Tips to help you cut down on fatty foods

- Grill, steam, or bake food instead of frying or roasting.
- Choose lean cuts of meat and use chicken, turkey, or fish instead of red meats.

- Go easy on fried foods, sausages, pies, biscuits, and cakes.
- Use skimmed or semi-skimmed milks and lower fat cheeses.

Children need plenty of energy for growth, so as you cut down on fat, it is important to eat more foods such as bread, pasta, vegetables, and fruit.

How can you choose polyunsaturated fats?

- Generally, animal fats contain more saturated fats. Foods made from animal fats such as butter, lard, and suet are high in saturated fats.
- Vegetable oils and fish oils and fats contain more polyunsaturated fats. So does white meat such as chicken and turkey.
- Hard margarines, even though they are made from vegetable or fish oils, are high in saturated fats. During manufacture the hardening process changes the fat to saturated fat.

[Q] How could you reduce the amount of fatty food that you eat? Use the 'Tips to help you cut down on fatty foods' to give you ideas.

Should we use butter, margarine, or oil in cooking?

food value in 100g	butter	hard margarine -animal and vegetable oil	sunflower margarine	sunflower oil
energy in kcal	740	730	730	900
fat	82g	81g	81g	100g
polyunsaturated fatty acids	2·2g	13g	60g	52g
saturated fatty acids	49g	30g	19g	13g

[Q] Use the chart above to help you.
1 What is the difference between butter, margarine, and oil?
2 Health experts suggest that we cut down on the amount of saturated fatty acids in our diet. Which fat should we cut down on, and which fat contains the lowest amount of saturated fatty acids?

Why has butter been used in some recipes in this book?
- The **flavour** of butter is different to that of margarine or oil. For recipes such as Potato Cakes and Cauliflower Cheese, we preferred the taste of butter, but you can use margarine and oil just as well.
- Butter can be used with oil for frying, as it improves the flavour, and helps fry food better than some margarines.

In general, polyunsaturated margarines and cooking oils have been chosen for recipes.

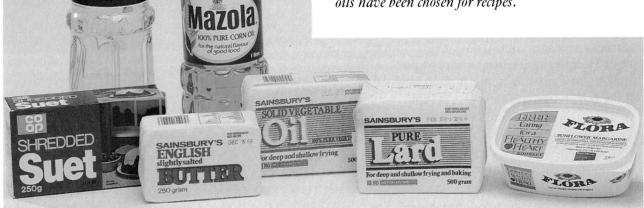

Which milk should you choose?

Use the chart to answer the questions:

Food value in 570 ml (1 pint)	Whole milk	Semi-skimmed milk	Skimmed milk
Total fat	22.2 g	10.5 g	0.6 g
Saturated fat	13.2 g	6.3 g	0.3 g
Energy kcal	380	280	195
Protein	19.3 g	19.5 g	19.9 g
Calcium	702 mg	729 mg	761 mg
Vit B$_2$	1.11 mg	1.12 mg	1.17 mg
Vit A	228 μg	104 μg	Trace
Vit D	0.13 μg	0.05 μg	Trace

Source: National Dairy Council

1 As part of a healthy eating plan, we should cut down on the amount of fat we eat. Recipes in this book use **skimmed milk**. Why has this milk been chosen?
2 Apart from the fat content, is there much difference between whole, semi-skimmed, and skimmed milk? If so, what is the difference?
3 Milk is an important food as it provides valuable nutrients, especially **calcium**, for bones and teeth. Is the amount of calcium in each milk very different?
4 The Government recommend that children under five years should not drink skimmed milk because of its lower energy value (kilocalories) and vitamin A content. Explain how the chart gives this information.

Cooking matters!

You can alter the fat content of food by the way you cook it.

Look at this chart for cooked potatoes:

Food value in 100 g type of potato	kcal	fat content
boiled potato	80	0.1 g
mashed potato	119	5.0 g
baked potato	105	0.1 g
roast potato	157	4.8 g
chips	253	10.9 g
crisps	533	35.9 g

Q 1 How can you explain the increase in the amount of fat between **a** baked and roast potatoes **b** boiled and mashed potatoes **c** chips and crisps?
2 Which method of cooking is the healthiest? Give your reasons.

Low fat products

More and more food manufacturers are producing low fat foods and sales are increasing every year. These foods include low fat spreads, cheeses, yoghurt, and milk.

1 Study the three labels below. They compare Shape low fat products with other dairy products.

a Copy this table and fill it in to show the difference in the amount of fat in each food.

	amount of fat in 100 g
Shape low fat soft cheese	8.8 g
cream cheese	
full fat soft cheese	
Shape low fat cheese	
Cheddar cheese	
Shape low fat yoghurt	
standard low fat yoghurt	

b Draw a bar chart to show the different amounts of fat in each food.

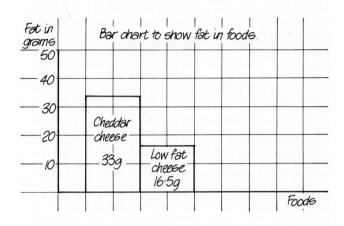

2 Why do some people buy low fat products? Give an example of the type of person who might choose them and say why.

3 How can we cut down on the amount of fat in our diet without buying special low fat foods?

St. Ivel Shape – the first British range of low fat dairy products to help you and your family to eat well and stay in shape.
St. Ivel Shape Low Fat Soft Cheese is made with pure dairy ingredients to give you all the luxury of cream cheese but less than half the fat.
It has far fewer calories than either cream cheese or full fat soft cheese.

Shape Low Fat Soft Cheese
Less than half the fat of Cream Cheese

per 100g	Shape	Cream Cheese	Full Fat Soft Cheese
Fat	8.8g	46.0g	21.0g
Cals	135	450	255
Protein	12.6g	7.0g	15.5g

Shape Low Fat Soft Cheese freezes well
For best results after freezing stir before serving

Less than half the fat of Cream Cheese

St. Ivel Shape – the first British range of low fat dairy products to help you and your family to eat well and stay in shape.
St. Ivel Shape fruit yogurts have a fresh and creamy taste but contain only half the fat and calories of standard low fat yogurts.
Enjoy your favourite fruit yogurt flavours – strawberry, raspberry, peach melba and black cherry – and save on fat and calories too.

Shape Yogurt
Less than half the fat of standard low fat yogurt

per 100g	Shape	Standard Low Fat Yogurt
Fat	0.2g	1g
KCalories	41	90
Protein	4.8g	4.8g
Carbohydrate	5.5g	16.5g

Less than half the fat but all the taste

St. Ivel Shape – the first British range of low fat dairy products to help you and your family to eat well and stay in shape.
St. Ivel Shape Cheese is made with pure dairy ingredients to give you a cheese with all the taste of Cheddar but only half the fat.
Because Shape Cheese is low in fat, it is also low in calories containing just 77 calories an ounce – that's fewer than any other traditional hard cheese – even Edam.

Shape Cheese
Half the fat of Cheddar

per 100g	Shape	Cheddar
Fat	16.5g	33.1g
Calories	270	405
Protein	27.1g	26.8g

Shape Cheese freezes well

Half the fat of Cheddar

What is a low fat cheese?

A low fat cheese is made from skimmed or semi-skimmed milk instead of whole milk.

e Try making a low fat soft cheese. You can use the cheese in some of the recipes in this book, or eat it with salad or in sandwiches.

You need:

600 ml milk –
  skimmed or
  semi-skimmed
2–3 tablespoons
  lemon juice
pinch of salt
saucepan

thermometer
bowl
sieve
muslin or J-cloth
  and string
spoon
dish

1 Heat the milk in a saucepan to 38°C.
2 Pour into a bowl, stir in lemon juice and leave for 15 minutes. Write down what happens.
3 Put a wet J-cloth or piece of muslin into a sieve and place over a bowl.
4 Strain the milk through the sieve. The **curds** (solid part) stay in the sieve, and the **whey** (liquid part) runs into the bowl.
5 Tie up the cloth or muslin and leave to drain for 30–40 minutes.
6 Weigh the curd and measure the whey, then put the curd into a dish, stir in a little salt, and taste your cheese.

Copy and fill in the chart with your results:

amount of milk	600 ml
what happens when lemon juice is added?	
weight of curd (solid part)	
weight of whey (liquid part)	
taste	

Q 1 How much soft cheese is made from 600 ml milk?
2 Why does 100 g of soft cheese contain more protein and fat than 100 g (100 ml) of the milk from which it was made?
3 Which milk would make a soft cheese with the lowest fat content: skimmed or semi-skimmed milk? Explain your answer.

Salt

Salt is the name for the chemical compound **Sodium chloride**. Salt is essential in our diet to control the fluid balance in our bodies and maintain normal blood pressure. Too much salt in our diet may lead to high blood pressure, so some experts recommend that we should eat less salt.

No one is sure how much salt we actually need each day. Estimates vary from 2–8 g daily.

Many savoury recipes in this book use salt. Salt adds flavour to bland foods such as beans, rice, and root vegetables. To control the amount of salt you eat:

● only add a very little during cooking
● do not put the salt pot on the table at meal times
● in recipes, don't add extra salt if salty foods such as canned beans, bacon or ham are used
● try using other flavourings such as pepper, herbs, garlic or lemon juice
● cut down on salty snacks such as crisps and peanuts.

Sugar in food

Health experts recommend that we cut down on the amount of sugar we eat. Sugary foods are known to cause tooth decay.

Sugars occur naturally in foods. Fructose is a type of sugar found in fruit, and lactose is a sugar found in milk. Although fruits and milk contain a little natural sugar, they also provide us with other valuable nutrients such as vitamin C and calcium. Sucrose is found in sugar beet and sugar cane. It is extracted from these plants as white or brown sugar, treacle, and golden syrup. Sucrose is 100% sugar and contains no other valuable nutrients. Golden syrup is 80% sugar, the rest being made up of water.

We can try to cut down on the amount of sugar (sucrose) that we eat by adding less to drinks such as tea, and less to food during cooking. However, sugar is often added to food during processing. The chart shows a list of foods which have had sugar added to them during manufacture. This includes all types of sugars and sugar syrups that may be used. Naturally occurring sugars, such as fructose and lactose, which may be found in these foods, have not been included in these figures.

food	g of sugar added to 100 g of food
cola and fizzy drinks	6.7 g
honey and nut cornflakes	36.2 g
digestive biscuits	20.0 g
baked beans	4.3 g
cream of tomato soup	4.3 g
ice cream	22.0 g
canned peaches in syrup	10.0 g
dolly mixtures	83.0 g
cornflakes	6.5 g
tomato ketchup	17.2 g

Source: Tesco Guide to Nutrition

Q 1 List the foods which contain more added sugar than you expected.

2 What healthier alternatives could you choose to eat or drink instead of **a** cola and fizzy drinks **b** sugary breakfast cereals **c** canned peaches in syrup?
3 If one teaspoon of sugar weighs 5 g, how many teaspoons of sugar, approximately, are added to:
a 100 g canned peaches in syrup **b** 100 g tomato ketchup **c** 100 g dolly mixtures?
4 How could you cut down on the amount of sugar that you eat?

Which flour should you use?

Food value in 100 g of food

	wholemeal flour	white flour
kcal	320	340
protein	13 g	11.0 g
fat	2 g	1.2 g
calcium	35 mg	40.0 g
iron	4 mg	2.0 mg
fibre	10 mg	4.0 g

Source: Bender and Bender

Q 1 Which flour contains the most **a** fibre **b** calcium **c** protein?
2 Which foods do you prefer – those made with wholemeal flour such as wholemeal bread, or those made with white flour? Can you give your reasons?

Flour and bread are valuable foods in the British diet. Health experts recommend that we increase the amount of dietary fibre in our food and more people are choosing wholemeal flour and wholemeal bread – but white flour is a nutritious food too. Some people like the taste and texture of foods made with white flour, such as white bread. For this reason some of the recipes in this book use white flour, others wholemeal. If you wish to change flours, use the same weight of flour, but use more water or liquid with wholemeal flour and less with white.

Fresh food is best

Fresh food is usually best for taste and food value. Fruits and vegetables lose flavour and valuable nutrients, especially vitamin C, once they are harvested. If food is eaten too long after its 'sell by' date, then it could also be a danger to our health.

Vitamin C content in raw potatoes mg per 100 g	
Newly harvested	30 mg
October–November	20 mg
December	15 mg
January–February	10 mg
March onwards	8 mg

Source: Potato Marketing Board

Q 1 Use the chart to explain what happens to the vitamin C content once potatoes are harvested.
2 When is the best time to buy British potatoes?
3 Potatoes are a good source of vitamin C in the British diet. How can you explain this?

Food additives

Many ready-prepared foods contain additives which are used for colouring, flavouring, and preserving food. The additives used in foods have been tested for safety and most are listed with E numbers on packets and cans. Not all scientists agree that all food additives are completely safe. A small number of people are allergic to food additives and for them certain foods can cause skin rashes or asthma.

Use the chart below to answer the questions.

food	no artificial colour	no additives
cod fish cakes	●	
100% beefburgers	●	
pork sausage meat		
cod steaks	●	●
smoked haddock		

● = no colour/no additives present in food

Source: Bejam

Q 1 Which food contains no artificial colour or additives?
2 Which foods contain artificial colour? Why do you think this is?
3 Which foods contain additives? What sort of additives are likely to be used? Collect real labels of the products or use leaflets and other textbooks to help you decide which additives might be used and why.
4 List ten foods which are free from artificial colour and additives.

⒤ Food tests

These three food tests can be carried out on food to find out whether the food contains fat, starch, or vitamin C. Do not carry out these tests in an area where food is being prepared for eating.

Test for fat

You need:

filter papers
teaspoons
cooking oil
water
foods to be tested

1 Put a few drops of oil on a piece of filter paper. Label it FAT.
2 Put some water on another piece and label it WATER.
3 Hold the filter papers up to the light. Both marks are slightly see-through, but the oil mark is greasy.
4 Leave both papers to dry. The oil will still leave a greasy mark.
5 Test other foods for fat. Press the foods on to the filter paper using the back of a teaspoon. Shake off the food and dry the paper.
6 Foods containing fat leave a greasy mark. Watery foods leave a stain which dries out.

Test for starch

You need:

saucers or testing
    tiles
iodine solution
dropper, pipette or
    spouted bottle
foods to test

1 Place a very small amount of food on a testing tile or saucer.
2 Add 1–2 drops of iodine solution to each food.
3 If starch is present, the colour will change to blue/black.
4 Remember: iodine is poisonous, so keep it away from food to be eaten, and wash your hands after using it.

Test for vitamin C

A blue chemical called PIDCP (formerly known as DCPIP) is used for this test. If vitamin C is present in food, the PIDCP changes from dark blue to colourless.

You need:

a little PIDCP powder mixed with 150 ml of cold water – mix up just before use in a beaker or flask
test tubes
test tube rack
dropper pipette
mortar and pestle
selection of foods for testing – especially fruit juice and squashes

1 Place about 1 cm of each food for testing in each test tube. Solid food needs grinding up, so use a mortar and pestle or chop up finely and mix with a little water.
2 Add the PIDCP drop by drop to the food in the test tubes. If vitamin C is present, the blue drops will become colourless.
3 You can count the number of drops of PIDCP you needed to add until the mixture turned blue once more. This is when all the vitamin C in the test tube has been used up. Compare the number of drops for each food. This will also help you compare the vitamin C content.

Make a list of all the foods that you test. Copy the chart below and fill in your results.

food	does it contain fat?	starch?	vitamin C?

ROOTS AND BULBS

The recipes in this section use roots and bulbs –
the part of the plant which grows on or below the ground.

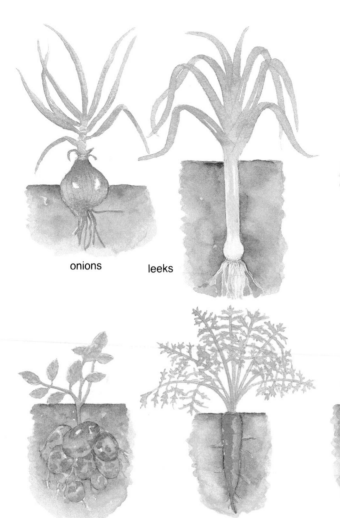

onions   leeks   garlic   beetroot

potatoes   carrots   sweet potato   parsnip

Q Sort through the recipes in this section and find
ten more roots or bulbs.

Food value

Roots such as potatoes, yams, and sweet potatoes
contain **starch**, a valuable source of **energy**. All
vegetables provide some **dietary fibre**, especially
in the outer skins of root vegetables. So
vegetables should be carefully peeled, or baked
in their 'jackets'.

Carrots and sweet potatoes contain **carotene**
which the body changes to **vitamin A** during
digestion. Vitamin A helps to keep us healthy and
helps us to see in dim light.

Roots and bulbs contain some **vitamin C**, but
often these vegetables are stored over winter, and
some vitamin C is lost during that time (see page
14).

Onions, leeks, and some roots contain a little
calcium, a mineral important for healthy teeth
and bones.

Food value chart

This chart shows the food value of 100 g of some root vegetables, plus fish and eggs:

	carrots (boiled)	potatoes (boiled)	onions (boiled)	sweet potatoes (boiled)	grilled fish	egg
energy value	20 kcal	80 kcal	10 kcal	85 kcal	100 kcal	150 kcal
protein	0.6 g	1.4 g	0.6 g	1 g	21 g	12.3 g
fat	–	–	–	0.6 g	1.3 g	10.9 g
carbohydrate	4 g	20 g	3 g	20 g	–	–
fibre	3 g	2 g	1 g	2 g	–	–
vitamin A	12000 µg	–	–	700 µg	–	140 µg
vitamin C	4 mg	10 mg	5 mg	15 mg	–	–
calcium	40 mg	–	25 mg	–	–	50
iron	0.4 mg	0.3 mg	0.3 mg	0.6 mg	0.4 mg	2 mg

Source: Bender and Bender

Q Use the food value chart to answer the following:

1 Explain the difference in food values between 100 g of:
   a eggs and carrots
   b fish and potatoes
   c sweet potatoes and onions

2 Draw up a chart like the one below.
   Imagine that you had a meal of 100 g of grilled fish, 100 g of boiled potatoes, and 100 g of boiled carrots! Fill in the food values on the chart, then add up the totals.
   In a healthy diet, we should try to eat a variety of foods, which provide us with a variety of nutrients. Do you think this meal provides variety? (Is there a figure in each column?)

3 Use your answers for questions 1 and 2 to help answer the following:
   'What is the value of roots and bulbs as part of a healthy eating plan?'

	fish (100 g)	potatoes (100 g)	carrots (100 g)	TOTAL
energy value				
protein				
fat				
carbohydrate				
fibre				
vitamin A				
vitamin C				
calcium				
iron				

17

How much of a vegetable is wasted?

Some root vegetables with tough skins must be peeled. Others, such as potatoes and carrots, may be scrubbed clean and eaten in their skins. In this way some of the dietary fibre and vitamin C is saved.

How much of a root vegetable is peeled away?

Weigh the peelings after you have prepared a root vegetable from this recipe section. Copy the chart below and work out the percentage waste.

How to work out percentage waste

If 110 g of parsnip is peeled and the peelings weigh 25 g, what percentage is the waste?

$$\text{Percentage waste} = \frac{\text{weight of peelings}}{\text{weight of parsnip}} \times 100$$

So for the parsnip $\frac{25}{110} \times 100 = 22.7\%$ waste or about 23%

Q 1 Why do you peel off more skin from some vegetables than others?
2 How could this waste be cut down? Remember you could use different knives and peelers.

Which is best – boiling, steaming, or microwave cooking?

Which of these three methods cooks root vegetables the fastest and which gives the best results?

i Each cooking method is investigated by a separate group.

Each group needs:
a small potato or other root vegetable weighing about 100 g	knife chopping board sieve
stop watch or timer	plate

1 Wash the potato. Without peeling it, cut into 1 cm cubes.
2 Cook each potato for five minutes by one of the methods below.

Boiling
Half-fill a pan with boiling water, then boil the potato for five minutes.
Drain and put on a plate immediately.

Steaming
Put a steamer or sieve over a pan of boiling water and cook the potato for five minutes, then serve on the plate.

Microwave cooking
Put the potato in a small bowl, cover with boiling water and cook in the microwave for five minutes. Drain and serve.

Taste the three samples. Notice the difference in colour and texture of the potato cubes. Were they soft, firm, or crumbly?

Copy this chart and fill in your results.

cooking method	colour	texture
boiling		
steaming		
microwave		

Use the potato to make Potato Salad. Mix with a little mayonnaise and yoghurt.

1 Which method was the quickest, and which gave the best results? Try and explain your answers.

2 Why is it important to cut all the cubes to the same size? Why do most recipes cook potatoes for 20 minutes, yet these took only five minutes?

Dietary fibre and cellulose cell walls

Dietary fibre, which helps keep the gut healthy, is found in the cell walls of plants in the form of cellulose. If the skin of onions is peeled very thinly, these cellulose cell walls can easily be seen using a microscope. The red variety of onions give a very good result.

You need:

red or white onion
sharp knife
glass slide with cover slip
microscope with ×100 magnification

1 Cut into the onion and carefully remove a thin strip of red or clear skin from an inner moist layer.
2 Place this strip on a microscope slide. Add a drop of water to keep the onion moist and cover with the cover slip.
3 Examine the onion cells under a microscope using ×100 magnification.
4 Draw the results. You will see a collection of six-sided cells, with colourless cell walls. If red onion is used, the inside of the cells and the cell walls are red and so easier to see.

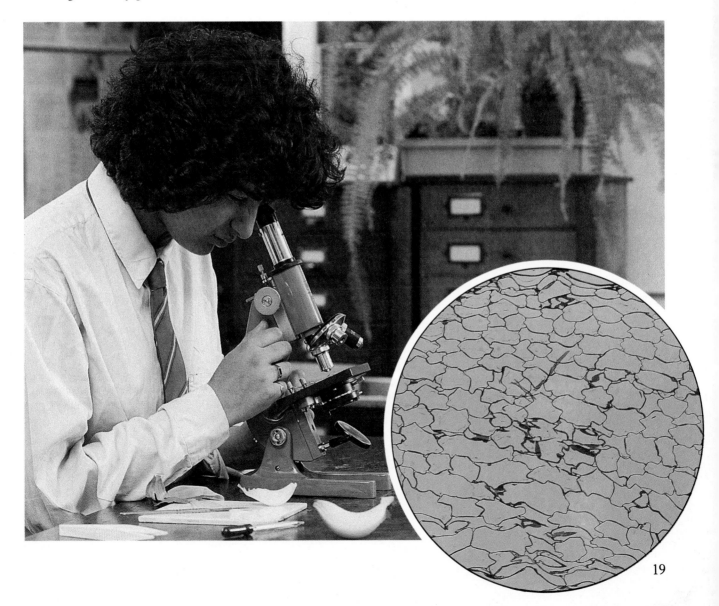

◆ DO IT YOURSELF SOUP ◆

Soups can be made from almost any vegetable but the root vegetables are particularly good for winter soups. Use an onion and a carrot as a base and then choose the major ingredient yourself.

1 tbs polyunsaturated cooking oil
1 onion, peeled and chopped (100 g)
1 carrot, peeled and chopped (100 g)
300 g root vegetable, peeled and chopped
700 ml water
vegetable *or* chicken stock cube
salt and pepper

tablespoon	kitchen knife
wooden spoon	sieve or food
chopping board	processor

1 Heat the oil in a pan and very gently fry the onion for 1–2 minutes.
2 Add the carrot and your chosen vegetable and continue frying gently for a further 2–3 minutes.
3 Add all the remaining ingredients and bring to the boil. Cover and simmer for 30 minutes.
4 Rub through a sieve or purée in a blender or food processor.

Serves 4.   *Cooking time: 35 minutes.*

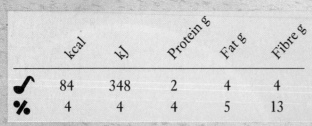

	kcal	kJ	Protein g	Fat g	Fibre g
🥄	84	348	2	4	4
%	4	4	4	5	13

(Calculated for parsnips)

◆ LEEK AND POTATO SOUP ◾

This makes a hearty winter soup, which can be liquidized to a smooth soup using a liquidizer or processor.

1 small onion, peeled and chopped (50 g)
400 g leeks, cleaned and sliced (300 g)
400 g potatoes, peeled and cubed
600 ml chicken stock (600 ml + chicken stock cube)
100 ml skimmed milk
black pepper

kitchen knife	measuring jug
chopping board	saucepan with lid

1 Place all the ingredients in a saucepan and cover with a lid.
2 Bring gently to the boil and simmer for 20 minutes.

Serves 4.   *Cooking time: 20 minutes.*

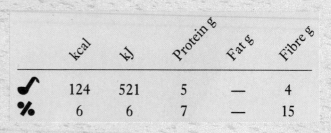

	kcal	kJ	Protein g	Fat g	Fibre g
🥄	124	521	5	—	4
%	6	6	7	—	15

◆ RAW ROOT SALAD ◆

Raw grated carrot is often used in salads but other raw vegetables can also be served in this way. Find as many different coloured root vegetables as you can to make an attractive display. Do not use potatoes.

Approximately 450 g root and other vegetables such as beetroot, carrot, celeriac, turnip, kholrabi, swede, radish, Jerusalem artichoke
lemon juice
salad oil
lettuce leaves, endive *or* chicory to garnish

kitchen knife   bowls
peeler   plate
grater

1 Peel the vegetables and grate into individual bowls.
2 Add lemon juice to those which may discolour such as carrot or Jerusalem artichoke and a very little oil to each one to keep it from drying out.
3 Arrange spoonfuls in an attractive pattern on a plate and garnish with shredded lettuce leaves, endive or chicory.

Serves 4.

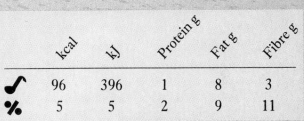

	kcal	kJ	Protein g	Fat g	Fibre g
🎵	96	396	1	8	3
%	5	5	2	9	11

Good source of vitamin A

◆ ALL-CHANGE POTATO SALAD ■

Cold cooked potatoes can be turned into a variety of tasty and colourful dishes just by tossing them in a different dressing or adding an extra flavouring ingredient or two. Here's a start; see if you can think of any more ideas.

600 g potatoes, cooked, peeled and diced
salt and pepper

Flavourings
3–4 spring onions, finely chopped
2 tbs freshly chopped parsley
1 tsp whole coriander seeds, toasted under the grill and crushed
1 tsp freshly chopped mint
¼ green pepper, very finely chopped
1 stick celery, very finely chopped

Dressings
4 tbs vinaigrette made with olive *or* salad oil and cider *or* wine vinegar
3 tbs mayonnaise *or* salad cream
3 tbs soured cream *or* Greek yoghurt

kitchen knife   chopping board
tablespoon   mixing bowl
fork

1 Place potatoes in a bowl with the seasonings and add one or two of the flavourings, such as onion and parsley, crushed coriander, or green pepper and celery.
2 Spoon on your chosen dressing and toss everything together.

Serves 4.

	kcal	kJ	Protein g	Fat g	Fibre g
🥄	221	931	4	8	4
%	10	10	7	9	12

Good source of vitamin C

◆ BEETROOT AND RAISIN SALAD ■

Try this attractive salad with both raw and cooked beetroot. It is very good either way.

225 g cooked *or* raw beetroot, peeled
3 spring onions, trimmed and sliced (35 g)
1 eating apple, cored and chopped (100 g)
50 g raisins
150 ml natural, low fat yoghurt
½–1 tsp grated horseradish *or* horseradish sauce
freshly grated black pepper

kitchen knife   chopping board
teaspoon   grater
tablespoon   mixing bowl

1 Grate the beetroot, using a fine cutter for raw beetroot and the coarse cutter for cooked beetroot, into a bowl.
2 Add the remaining ingredients and toss well together.

Serves 4.

	kcal	kJ	Protein g	Fat g	Fibre g
🥄	79	328	3	0.3	3
%	4	4	5	0.3	11

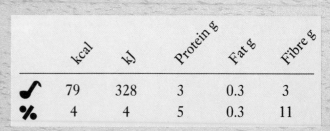

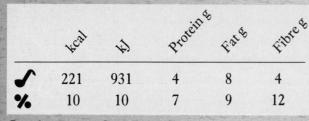

◆ SOUFFLE POTATOES ■

The potatoes can be cooked in the microwave in advance. Arrange in a circle and microwave four on full power for 15–17 minutes. Larger numbers will take longer.

4 × 170 g potatoes, cooked in their jackets
4 eggs, separated
salt and pepper
Choice of flavourings
8 rashers of bacon, crisply grilled and chopped
or
60 g grated cheese
or
1 × 225 g can baked beans

kitchen knife   egg whisk
fork   baking tray
grater   bowl
spoon

1 Set the oven to 200°C/400°F/Gas 6.
2 Cut the potatoes in half along their length and scoop out all the flesh, retaining the skins.
3 Mix the flesh with the egg yolks, seasoning and your chosen flavourings.
4 Whisk the egg whites until stiff and mix 2–3 tablespoons with the potato mixture. Fold in the rest of the egg white and spoon the mixture into the potato skins.
5 Place on a baking tray and bake for 20 minutes until set and golden.

Serves 4.   *Cooking time: 20 minutes.*

(Calculation for cheese)	kcal	kJ	Protein g	Fat g	Fibre g
♪	303	1274	15	12	3
%	14	14	28	14	11

Good source of vitamin A

◆ POTATO CAKES ■

Serve with butter or margarine as an alternative to bread. They are delicious with boiled or scrambled eggs.

500 g potatoes, which have been boiled in
their skins and peeled
salt
15 g butter *or* firm margarine
black pepper
50 g wholemeal flour

kitchen knife	saucepan
tablespoon or slotted	bowl
spoon	baking tray
potato masher	

1 Boil the potatoes in their skins in lightly salted water.
2 When they are cooked leave to cool a little and peel off the skins.

3 Set the oven to 200°C/400°F/Gas 6 and grease a baking tray.
4 Mash the potatoes with the butter or margarine and mix in the pepper and flour.
5 Shape into a very thin oval or square on the greased baking tray and mark into sections with a knife.
6 Bake for 30–35 minutes until well browned and crisp at the edges. Break into sections to serve.

Serves 4.   *Cooking time: 50 minutes.*

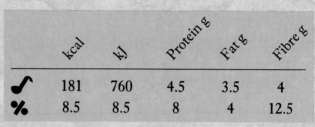

	kcal	kJ	Protein g	Fat g	Fibre g
🥄	181	760	4.5	3.5	4
%	8.5	8.5	8	4	12.5

Watch the fat!

◆ FISH BURGERS ■

Fish cakes are made the world over. In the West Indies salt cod is used to make 'Stamp and Go', in South America minced prawns are used to make spicy Bombas and in Europe fresh fish is used to make fish burgers.

300 g cooked white fish *or* soaked and cooked salt cod or minced cooked prawns
200 g cooked mashed potato *or* yams
1 egg, beaten
salt and pepper
cooking oil

Optional flavourings
50 g Cheddar Cheese, grated
or
1 tsp chilli powder
or
3 tbs freshly chopped parsley

teaspoon or tablespoon
fork
mixing bowl

baking tray
grater
pastry brush

1 Set oven to 220°C/425°F/Gas 7.
2 Mix the chosen fish in a bowl with the potato or yams, egg, seasonings and any optional flavourings.
3 Shape into 4 burgers and brush with a little cooking oil.
4 Place on a grill tray lined with foil or a baking tray and grill for 4–5 minutes on each side or bake for 15–20 minutes until golden in colour.

Serves 2.
Cooking time: 8–10 minutes or 20–30 minutes.

	kcal	kJ	Protein g	Fat g	Fibre g
♪	375	1566	43	13	2
%	17	17	81	16	7

Good source of calcium

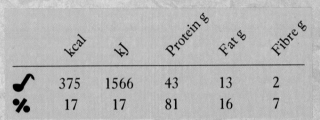

◆ GOLDEN ROOT BAKE ■

This recipe uses both swedes and turnips. In the North of England and in Scotland, the two vegetables often swap names.

150 g small white turnips, peeled and chopped
100 g yellow swede, peeled and chopped
salt
1 egg, separated
freshly ground pepper
nutmeg

kitchen knife	small saucepan with lid
potato masher	whisk
fork	2 small ovenproof dishes

1 Place the vegetables in a pan and cover with water. Season and bring to the boil.
2 Cover and simmer for 25 minutes until tender.
3 Set the oven to 190°C/375°F/Gas 5 and grease 2 small ovenproof dishes.
4 Drain the vegetables well and mash with a potato masher. Add the salt, pepper and nutmeg.
5 Whisk the egg white stiffly and fold into the purée. Spoon into the greased dishes. Beat the egg yolks and pour over the top.
6 Bake for 15 minutes.

Serves 2.   *Cooking time: 15 minutes.*

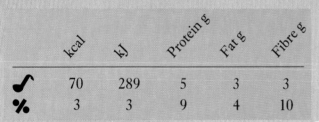

	kcal	kJ	Protein g	Fat g	Fibre g
♪	70	289	5	3	3
%	3	3	9	4	10

■ CHICKEN AND CARROT LOAF ■

Any strong flavoured vegetable could be used instead of carrot. Why not experiment with celery or beetroot?

150 g chopped *or* minced chicken thigh meat (4 thighs)
2 carrots, grated (approximately 100 g)
50 g fresh wholemeal breadcrumbs
1 small onion, grated (approximately 100 g)
1 egg, beaten
1 tsp freshly chopped basil *or* parsley

kitchen knife	fork
chopping board	tablespoon
grater	mixing bowl
teaspoon	450 g loaf tin

1 Set the oven to 190°C/375°F/Gas 5.
2 Place the chicken in a bowl with all the remaining ingredients and mix very well together.
3 Spoon the mixture into a loaf tin and bake in the oven for 50 minutes. Turn out and serve and cut into thick slices.

Serves 4.   *Cooking time: 50 minutes.*

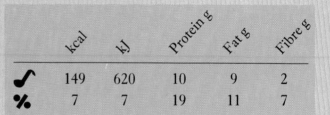

	kcal	kJ	Protein g	Fat g	Fibre g
♪	149	620	10	9	2
%	7	7	19	11	7

Good source of vitamin A

◆ CARROT MOUSSE ◆

This recipe is best cooked in a microwave oven but it can be cooked in an ordinary oven set at 190°C/375°F/Gas 5 for 1–1¼ hours.

450 g carrots, peeled and thinly sliced
salt
2 eggs, beaten
1 tbs plain flour (15 g)
50 ml skimmed milk
¼ tsp dried tarragon
salt and pepper

kitchen knife
fork
tablespoon
teaspoon

large basin
sieve, blender *or*
  food processor
small basin

1 Place the carrots in a bowl and cover with boiling water and microwave on full power for 15 minutes.
2 Drain the carrots and rub through a sieve or process in a blender or food processor.
3 Mix in all the remaining ingredients and spoon into a pudding basin.
4 Microwave on full power for 9–10 minutes until the mousse is set in the centre. Leave to stand for 3 minutes. Turn out and serve cut into wedges.

Serves 4.   *Cooking time: 25 minutes (microwave).*

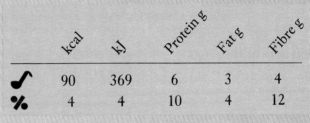

	kcal	kJ	Protein g	Fat g	Fibre g
♪	90	369	6	3	4
%	4	4	10	4	12

Good source of vitamin A

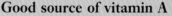

◆ FOUR VEGETABLE DISH WITH GINGER

You can vary the vegetables in this recipe according to the seasons. The following recipe is suitable for the winter months.

2 tbs polyunsaturated cooking oil
100 g carrots (approx) peeled and sliced
100 g celeriac or parsnips, peeled and sliced
1 medium-sized onion, skinned and sliced
3 cm piece fresh root ginger, peeled and cut into thin slivers
½ green pepper, seeded and thinly sliced
4 tbs soy sauce
1 tsp cornflour
4 tbs chicken stock

kitchen knife   teaspoon
wooden spoon   frying pan *or* wok
tablespoon

1 Cut the carrots and celeriac into thin matchsticks.
2 Heat the oil in the wok and stir-fry the carrots and celeriac for 2 minutes. Add the onions, ginger and green pepper and stir-fry for a further 1½ minutes.
3 Mix the cornflour and stock to a smooth cream, stir in the soy sauce and add to the frying pan or wok.
4 Bring the mixture to the boil and simmer for 2–3 minutes until the root vegetables have softened but are still slightly crunchy to the bite.

Serves 4.   *Cooking time: 6–6½ minutes.*

	kcal	kJ	Protein g	Fat g	Fibre g
♪	112	465	2	8	2
%	5	5	3	9	7

◆ GINGER CARROT BREAD

Grate the carrot as finely as you can and squeeze out any excess moisture with your fingers before using.

200 g carrots, very finely grated
200 g wholemeal flour
2 tsp baking powder
1 tsp ground ginger
¼ tsp ground cinnamon
50 ml skimmed milk
1 egg, beaten

grater   mixing bowl
teaspoon   450 g loaf tin

1 Set the oven to 230°C/450°F/Gas 8.
2 Place all the ingredients in a mixing bowl and knead well together with your fingers.
3 Transfer to a loaf tin and bake for 10 minutes.
4 Reduce the heat to 190°C/375°F/Gas 5 and bake for a further hour. Turn out onto wire rack and leave to cool.

Makes 1 × 450 g loaf. Serves 10.

Cooking time: 1 hr 10 minutes.

	kcal	kJ	Protein g	Fat g	Fibre g
♪	70	295	3	0.4	3
%	3	3	5	0.5	9

Good source of vitamin A

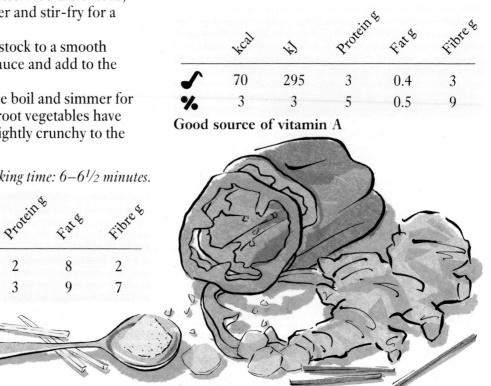

◆ PARSNIP PIE ◆

Any kind of root vegetable can be used as a topping in this way but the flavour of parsnips, celeriac, and Jerusalem artichokes work particularly well.

250 g lean minced beef
1 onion, peeled and sliced
1 tbs tomato purée
1 tbs cornflour
1 × 213 g can butter beans
salt and pepper
450 g parsnips, peeled and cubed
25 g margarine
50 g fresh wholemeal breadcrumbs

kitchen knife   ovenproof dish
tablespoon   chopping board
wooden spoon   masher
2 saucepans

1 Fry the mince in a pan to release the fat. Drain off any excess and add the onions. Continue frying for 3–4 minutes.
2 Stir in the tomato purée and cornflour and then add the liquid from the can of beans.
3 Bring the mixture to the boil stirring all the time and when it thickens stir in the beans.
4 Cook the parsnips in a very little lightly salted boiling water for 20 minutes until tender.
5 Set the oven to 200°C/400°F/Gas 6.
6 Spoon the beef and bean mixture into an ovenproof dish.
7 Drain the parsnips and mash well. Stir in the margarine and breadcrumbs and spoon over the top of the pie.
8 Bake for 25 minutes until the topping is golden and crisp.

Serves 4.   *Cooking time: 45 minutes.*

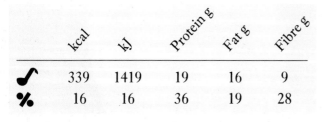

	kcal	kJ	Protein g	Fat g	Fibre g
✓	339	1419	19	16	9
%	16	16	36	19	28

◆ POTATO AND CELERIAC QUICHE ◆

The potato pastry used in this quiche can be used for any kind of savoury flan. For the best results, chill the pastry for half an hour before cooking.

Pastry
50 g firm margarine
75 g cold cooked and mashed potato
100 g wholemeal flour
1 tsp baking powder
pinch of salt
Filling
200 g celeriac, peeled and sliced
3 eggs, beaten
150 ml Greek yoghurt
50 ml skimmed milk
75 g cheese
salt and pepper

teaspoon   mixing bowl
fork   20 cm flan tin *or* flan ring
grater   and baking tray

1 Set the oven to 190°C/375°F/Gas 5.
2 Cream the margarine and use a fork to work in the cold potato, flour, baking powder and salt. Blend well and turn out onto floured surface.
3 Knead lightly and roll out to fill the base of a 20 cm loose-based flan tin. Work the pastry up the sides of the flan with your fingers and if time allows place in fridge for ½ hour.
4 Cook the celeriac in boiling water for 10 minutes. Drain and grate.
5 Beat the eggs, yoghurt and milk together and stir in the cheese, celeriac, and seasoning.
6 Spoon into the flan base, spread evenly and bake for about 45 minutes until set in the centre and golden brown.

Serves 4.   *Cooking time: 45 minutes.*

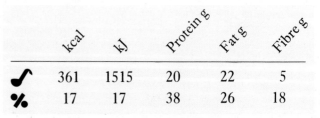

	kcal	kJ	Protein g	Fat g	Fibre g
✓	361	1515	20	22	5
%	17	17	38	26	18

◆ HARLEQUIN FISH PIE ◆

Choose any kind of white fish: haddock, cod, coley, huss, whiting or bream.

1 onion peeled and chopped
1 carrot, peeled and chopped
1 parsnip, peeled and chopped
350 ml milk
400 g white fish fillets, cut into chunks
50 g frozen peas
50 g frozen sweetcorn kernels *or*
canned sweetcorn
25 g firm margarine
25 g flour
black pepper
2–3 Weetabix *or* Shredded Wheat, crushed

kitchen knife   casserole or pie dish
2 small saucepans   chopping board
tablespoon   wooden spoon
teaspoon   measuring jug
wire whisk

1 Pour the milk over the onion, carrot and parsnip in a small saucepan and bring very carefully to the boil.

2 Reduce the heat, simmer for 10 minutes then drain the liquid into a jug.
3 Set the oven to 190°C/375°F/Gas 5 and grease a pie dish.
4 Mix the fish with the cooked and frozen vegetables and spoon into the pie dish.
5 Heat the margarine with the flour and reserved cooking liquid. Beat with a wire whisk until the mixture boils and thickens. Season and cook for 3–4 minutes and then pour over the fish and vegetables.
6 Top with crushed cereals and bake for 30–35 minutes until the fish is cooked through and crisp on top.

Serves 4.   *Cooking time: 50 minutes.*

	kcal	kJ	Protein g	Fat g	Fibre g
♪	364	1265	25	7	6
%	14	14	47	8	19

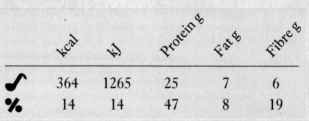

◆ CHEESE AND ONION ROLL ■

This dish is equally delicious hot or cold.

75 g wholemeal flour
75 g white flour
salt
60 g hard margarine *or* polyunsaturated lard
2–3 tbs water
25 g Edam cheese, grated
150 g Farmhouse Cheddar, grated
1 onion, peeled and chopped (70 g)
2 tbs tomato purée
pepper

kitchen knife   mixing bowl
tablespoon   baking tray
grater   chopping board

1 Place the flour and salt in a bowl and rub in the fat until the mixture resembles fine breadcrumbs.
2 Add the water and mix to a stiff dough with your fingers. Place in the fridge until required.
3 Mix all the remaining ingredients in a bowl.

4 Set the oven to 200°C/400°F/Gas 6.
5 Roll out the pastry to make a rectangle about 40 cm × 30 cm.
6 Spread the tomato purée and cheese mixture over the pastry leaving a small gap round the edges.
7 Roll up the pastry until it looks rather like a Swiss roll and place on a baking tray. Bend the roll round to make a semi-circle and then cut across the roll leaving the pastry uncut at the side inside the semi-circle to make about 8–10 sections.
8 Twist each cut section to lie almost on its side exposing the Swiss roll effect.
9 Bake for 25 minutes until golden in colour.

Serves 4.   *Cooking time: 25 minutes.*

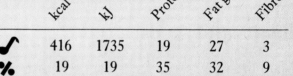

	kcal	kJ	Protein g	Fat g	Fibre g
♪	416	1735	19	27	3
%	19	19	35	32	9

Good source of vitamin A and calcium

BEANS, NUTS, AND SEEDS

In the past, beans, nuts, and other seeds were a valuable winter food store. They were dried before storing, and in the spring, any remaining seeds could be planted for a new food crop.

Beans and pulses are used in popular foods such as:

baked beans (haricot beans)

chilli con carne (red kidney beans)

dhal (lentils)

hummus (chickpeas)

Beans and seeds

Many beans, nuts, and seeds such as cereals are good sources of protein. The main function of protein is to build and repair the body cells. Beans and seeds contain dietary fibre which animal foods do not, and they contain less fat than eggs, milk, and cheese. For vegetarians who do not eat meat, beans, nuts, and seeds are useful foods.

Look at the amount of protein in 100 g of each of these foods:

food	grams of protein
peanuts	24
wholemeal bread	9
Cheddar cheese	26
eggs	12
peas	6
milk	3.4
baked beans	5
lentils	8
minced beef	19
fish fingers	13

Source: Bender and Bender

1 List the plant foods in order of their protein content.
2 List the animal foods in order of their protein content.
3 Beans and seeds add variety to our diet. They also cost less than most animal foods. Suggest two interesting ways of serving beans with other foods to make a meal. For example, chilli con carne is a meal of kidney beans and minced beef.

34

Fats and oils in seeds

Seeds from soya beans, peanuts and sunflowers are rich sources of fat, which manufacturers can extract and use for vegetable oils and fats.

Each of these seeds is used for cooking oils:

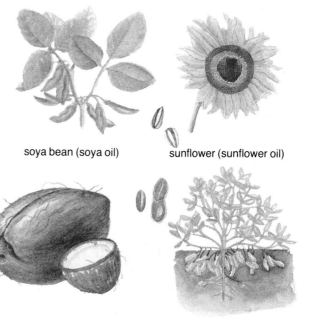

soya bean (soya oil)   sunflower (sunflower oil)

oil palm (palm oil)   rape seed (rape seed oil)   coconut (coconut oil)   peanuts (groundnut oil)

Health experts suggest that we cut down the amount of fat we eat, especially saturated fat. To help improve our diet, some saturated fat should be replaced with polyunsaturated fat.

Amount of polyunsaturated and saturated fat in 100 g of food

food	polyunsaturated fat	saturated fat
lard	9%	42%
soya oil	59%	14%
sunflower oil	52%	13%
groundnut oil	20%	30%
coconut oil	2%	76%

Source: McCance and Widdowson

1 Use the chart and the label for rape seed oil. List the six fats in order of their polyunsaturated fat content.
2 Draw up a bar chart to show your results.

Bar chart to show polyunsaturated fats in foods

% polyunsaturated fat

80%
60%
40%
20%

fats

3 Which of the six fats would you choose for a healthy diet? Give your reasons.
4 Why is coconut oil not recommended as part of a healthy eating plan?

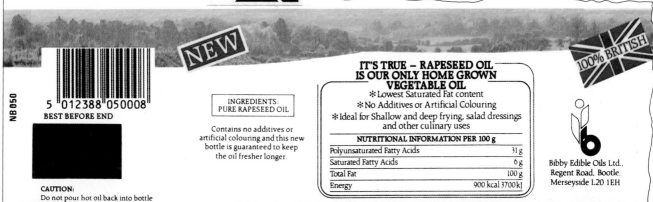

GOLDEN FIELDS PURE RAPESEED OIL

1 LITRE e   100% BRITISH

NB 050

BEST BEFORE END

5 012388 050008

NEW

INGREDIENTS:
PURE RAPESEED OIL

Contains no additives or artificial colouring and this new bottle is guaranteed to keep the oil fresher longer.

CAUTION:
Do not pour hot oil back into bottle

IT'S TRUE – RAPESEED OIL IS OUR ONLY HOME GROWN VEGETABLE OIL
✳ Lowest Saturated Fat content
✳ No Additives or Artificial Colouring
✳ Ideal for Shallow and deep frying, salad dressings and other culinary uses

NUTRITIONAL INFORMATION PER 100 g

Polyunsaturated Fatty Acids	31 g
Saturated Fatty Acids	6 g
Total Fat	100 g
Energy	900 kcal 3700 kJ

100% BRITISH

Bibby Edible Oils Ltd.,
Regent Road, Bootle,
Merseyside L20 1EH

How can taste affect healthy eating?

The value of different foods in your diet depends upon how much you like to eat them. Find out which kind of pea you like best! Collect together some of the different kinds of pea on the chart – fresh, frozen, canned garden, processed, and marrowfat peas. Form a tasting panel to find out which kind of pea is the class favourite. You can taste the peas hot or cold.

kind of pea	colour	taste	mark out of 10
fresh			
frozen			
canned garden			
canned processed			
canned marrowfat			

Which is your favourite?
For each kind of pea, count up how many people voted it their favourite. Record your results on a bar chart.

Use the peas to make Green Goddess Dip or Pea Soup.

Is the food value of fresh, frozen, and canned peas different?

Look at the table showing the food value of different peas.

Food value for 100 g

	water	protein	fibre	vitamin C
fresh boiled	80 g	5 g	5 g	15 mg
frozen boiled	80 g	5 g	12 g	13 mg
canned garden	82 g	5 g	6 g	8 mg
canned processed	72 g	6 g	8 g	trace

Source: McCance and Widdowson

1 Which kind of peas do you like best?
2 Which kind of peas have the most **a** water **b** protein **c** fibre **d** vitamin C?
3 Use your answers to 1 and 2. If you were asked whether fresh, frozen, or canned peas were best, what would you reply? Use the chart to help with your answer.

Sprouted beans

Many kinds of beans and seeds can be sprouted to give fresh, young shoots. You can buy beansprouts, cress, and alfalfa from supermarkets, but you can also try growing your own.

You need:

some seeds such as chickpeas, mung beans, sunflower seeds or mustard and cress

sieve   bowl

J-cloth   elastic band

1 Line the sieve with a damp J-cloth and sprinkle 25 g of seeds over the top.
2 Secure another piece of cloth on top of the sieve with an elastic band.
3 Run cold water through the sieve and stand to drain over the bowl.
4 Rinse the seeds twice a day for several days until they sprout and grow to about 3 cm in length. Seeds sprout at different rates, and some may take a week or longer.
5 Remove the seed pods before using the sprouts. Weigh the beansprouts you have grown. Beansprouts are traditionally grown from mung beans. This table shows the food value for 100 g.

	mung beans, raw	beansprouts
kcal	230	20
protein	22 g	3.8 g
fat	1 g	0.2 g
dietary fibre	22 g	0.3 g
vitamin C	very little	19 mg

1 What quantity of beansprouts grew from your 25 g of beans?
2 Compare the food value of mung beans and beansprouts. Why do you think these figures are different?
3 In some countries, sprouted beans make a useful food when fresh vegetables are scarce. Which important nutrient increases when seeds are sprouted?

Coffee, chocolate, and carob

All three of these flavourings are made from beans. Coffee beans grow inside a 'cherry' and cocoa beans in large pods. Both types of bean are dried, then roasted to improve their colour and flavour. Carob powder is made from the locust bean. Carob is similar in flavour to chocolate but is free from the stimulant caffeine.

cocoa pod and beans

locust bean for carob

coffee beans

◆ HUMMUS ◼

This traditional Middle Eastern recipe uses Tahina. This is a paste made from crushed sesame seeds. It is usually served with a little olive oil on the top, raw vegetables and pitta bread.

1 × 430 g can chickpeas, drained
2 tbs Tahina paste
1 clove of garlic, peeled and crushed
juice of 1 lemon *or* 3 tbs lemon juice
salt
paprika pepper

tablespoon   lemon squeezer
kitchen knife   bowl
chopping board   sieve *or* food processor

1 Rub the chickpeas through a sieve or blend in a food processor.
2 Add all the remaining ingredients except the paprika and blend well together.
3 Spoon into a bowl and sprinkle with paprika pepper.

Serves 4.   *Cooking time: Nil.*

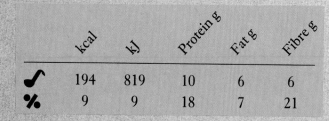

	kcal	kJ	Protein g	Fat g	Fibre g
🎵	194	819	10	6	6
%	9	9	18	7	21

◆ CHILLI BEAN DIP ◆

The more chilli powder you add the hotter it will be, so taste as you go. Serve with a selection of crisps, tortilla chips, and salt biscuits.

1 × 440 g can of red kidney beans, drained
½ small onion, grated (35 g)
¼ small green pepper, very finely chopped (30 g)
1 clove garlic, crushed
1 tbs tomato ketchup
75 g natural yoghurt
½ tsp ground chilli powder
salt and pepper

kitchen knife   sieve
tablespoon   bowl
teaspoon

Rub the beans through a sieve, or purée in a blender. Mix with all the remaining ingredients. Serve in a bowl.

Serves 8.   *Cooking time: Nil.*

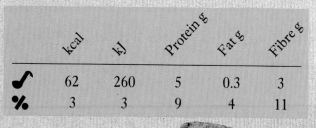

	kcal	kJ	Protein g	Fat g	Fibre g
🎵	62	260	5	0.3	3
%	3	3	9	4	11

◆ GREEN GODDESS DIP ■

Canned Pease Pudding can be used in this recipe in place of the marrowfat peas. The flavour is slightly different but it saves rubbing the peas through a sieve. Serve with a selection of raw vegetables.

1 × 284 g can marrowfat peas, drained
100 g low fat soft cheese such as quark or fromage frais
2 tbs skimmed milk
4 spring onions, very finely chopped
3 tbs freshly chopped parsley
1 tbs freshly chopped mint *or* ½ tsp dried mint
salt and freshly ground black pepper

tablespoon   sieve
kitchen knife   bowl

1 Rub the peas through a sieve or purée in a processor. Mix in all the remaining ingredients.
2 Add a little more milk if the mixture is too thick.
3 Spoon into a small bowl.

Serves 8.   *Cooking time: Nil.*

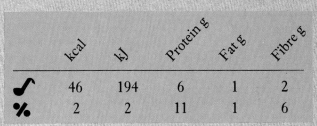

	kcal	kJ	Protein g	Fat g	Fibre g
♪	46	194	6	1	2
%	2	2	11	1	6

◆ CRUNCHY SPROUTED SALAD ■

Grow your own sprouted beans and seeds and use in this well-textured salad.

3 tbs alfalfa or cress (25 g)
2 tbs sprouted chickpeas *or* beansprouts (50 g)
1 tbs chopped walnuts (30 g)
1 tomato, chopped
5 cm piece cucumber, chopped
1 tsp lemon juice
1 tbs plain yoghurt (15 ml)

serving plate   kitchen knife
tablespoon   teaspoon

1 Spread the alfalfa or cress over the base of a small plate.
2 Mix the sprouted chickpeas with the walnuts, tomato and cucumber.
3 Toss in the lemon juice and yoghurt and pile onto the alfalfa or cress base.

Serves 1.   *Cooking time: Nil.*

	kcal	kJ	Protein g	Fat g	Fibre g
✔	219	911	11	16	8
%	10	10	22	20	26

Good source of vitamin C

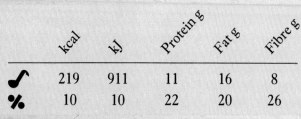

◆ GREEN PEA SOUP ■

Any kind of cooked or canned peas can be used in this recipe. You may need to add a little less liquid if you use mainly garden peas.

400 g cooked *or* canned peas, drained
1 chicken stock cube
300 ml water
100 ml milk
¼ tsp dried mixed herbs
freshly ground black pepper

food processor,   wooden spoon
  liquidizer or sieve teaspoon
measuring jug

1 Puree the peas or rub through a sieve.
2 Place in a pan with all the remaining ingredients and bring to the boil.
3 Simmer for 2–3 minutes to heat through and serve.

Serves 4.   *Cooking time: 2–3 minutes.*

	kcal	kJ	Protein g	Fat g	Fibre g
✔	78	325	7	0.4	2.5
%	4	4	13	0.5	8

◆ ITALIAN BEAN SALAD ◆

You can use striped pink borlotti beans or large whole haricot or cannellini beans in this recipe. Add the tuna for a main course dish and serve with a green salad.

1 × 430 g can pink or white beans, drained
½ small clove garlic, finely chopped
3 tbs freshly chopped parsley
1 × 200 g can tuna in brine, drained and flaked (optional)
2 tbs olive oil
1 tsp lemon juice *or* cider *or* wine vinegar
freshly ground black pepper
1 small onion, skinned and cut into thin rings (50 g)

kitchen knife
tablespoon
teaspoon

fork
bowl
chopping board

1 Mix the beans with the garlic and parsley. Add the flaked tuna, if using.
2 Pour on the oil and lemon juice or vinegar and toss the salad carefully.
3 Spoon the salad into a serving bowl or on to individual plates and top with the onion rings.

Serves 4.   *Cooking time: Nil.*

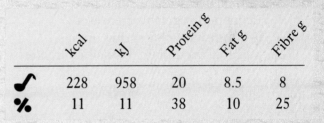

	kcal	kJ	Protein g	Fat g	Fibre g
🍴	228	958	20	8.5	8
%	11	11	38	10	25

◆ NUTTY ADVENTURE SALAD

Here's how to invent your own salad. Simply choose one or two items from each of the sections and toss them all together with a simple oil and vinegar dressing or a tablespoon or two of yoghurt and lemon juice.

green leaves:
lettuce, curly endive, watercress, chicory, rocket
1 tbs nuts:
peanuts, flaked Brazil nuts, chopped walnuts,
flaked almonds, chopped hazelnuts
chopped fruit in season:
half a green or red apple, a kiwi fruit,
half a peach or nectarine, a small pear, a tomato
chopped vegetable in season:
4–6 radishes, 2–3 spring onions,
5 cm piece of cucumber, 1 small courgette

kitchen knife   bowl
tablespoon

1 First choose your ingredients; six items will probably be more than enough.
2 Prepare the ingredients and toss well together in a bowl.
3 Add a simple dressing and serve at once with crusty wholemeal rolls.

Serves 1.   *Cooking time: Nil.*

	kcal	kJ	Protein g	Fat g	Fibre g
♪	152	637	7	13	4
%	7	7	13	15	12

(Estimated using lettuce and peanuts)

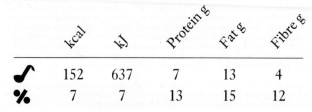

SOY PEANUT COOKIES

These crunchy cookies have a high protein content from the eggs, peanuts, and soy flour. Eat with a crisp apple and banana for a nutritional snack meal. Cookies are never as crisp as biscuits and the use of honey in place of sugar also makes them less crisp.

75 g runny honey
50 ml sunflower seed oil
1 large (size 1) egg, beaten
½ tsp salt
½ tsp ground coriander, cinnamon *or* allspice
50 g soy flour
110 g wholemeal flour
20 g peanuts, well chopped
cooking oil

teaspoon   bowl
fork   baking tray
dessertspoon   glass tumbler

1 Set the oven to 180°C/350°F/Gas 4.
2 Mix the honey and oil in a bowl and add the egg, salt and spices. Beat well with a fork.
3 Stir in the flours and nuts and mix to a stiff paste.
4 Drop dessertspoonfuls of the mixture into a lightly oiled baking tray. Flatten with the bottom of a glass dipped in water each time and make a criss-cross pattern with a fork on the top.
5 Bake for 15 minutes.

Makes 24.   *Cooking time: 15 minutes.*

	kcal	kJ	Protein g	Fat g	Fibre g
♪	61	255	2	3	0.7
%	3	3	4	4	2

Good source of iron

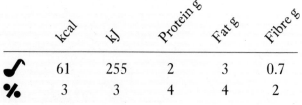

◆ BAKED APPLES WITH CRUNCHY CHOCOLATE FILLING ■

If you do not have any Muesli mix to hand, use large jumbo rolled oats.

2 large cooking apples (approx 300 g each)
15 g chocolate drops
10 g dry roasted peanuts, chopped
10 g Muesli mix
10 g raisins
2 tbs plain yoghurt

knife   tablespoon
apple corer   baking tray
basin   foil

1 Set the oven to 220°C/425°F/Gas 7.
2 Slit the skin of each apple all round the middle with a knife. Remove the core.

3 Mix all the remaining ingredients and spoon into the centre of the apples, pushing the mixture well down as you go.
4 Place on a shallow baking tray or ovenproof dish and bake covered in foil for 35 minutes.

Serves 2.   *Cooking time: 35 minutes.*

	kcal	kJ	Protein g	Fat g	Fibre g
✔	224	952	4	6	7
%	11	11	7	7	23

■ COFFEE AND CHOCOLATE MOUSSE ■

This interesting variation on chocolate mousse can be made with either cocoa or carob powder. Mocha is the name given to a mixture of coffee and chocolate flavours.

25 g cornflour
15 g cocoa or carob powder
300 ml skimmed milk
1 level tablespoon runny honey
1 heaped tsp instant coffee powder
4 glace cherries, cut in half

kitchen knife   measuring jug
teaspoon   basin
wooden spoon   saucepan

1　Blend the cornflour and carob powder with 4 tablespoons of milk in a large basin.
2　Heat the remaining milk in a pan with the honey and coffee powder, stirring until the honey has dissolved.
3　Just before the milk boils, pour over the cornflour mixture, stirring all the time.
4　Return the mixture to the pan and bring to the boil. Simmer for 3–4 minutes and remove from the heat. Place the pan in a basin of cold water and stir for 2–3 minutes to cool.
5　Spoon into a bowl and top with the cherries. Place in the fridge to set. Eat the same day.

Serves 4.
Cooking time: 3–4 minutes.

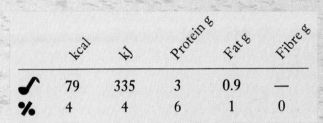

	kcal	kJ	Protein g	Fat g	Fibre g
🍴	79	335	3	0.9	—
%	4	4	6	1	0

Good source of calcium and iron

■ AMERICAN PEANUT BUTTER COOKIES ■

Peanuts are not really nuts. They belong in the pulse family and are rich in protein and fat. Peanut butter should be used sparingly. For the best results the dough should be chilled in the fridge before shaping into cookies.

75 g margarine
75 g crunchy peanut butter
50 g light Muscovado *or* brown sugar
1 egg, beaten
2 tsp milk
150 g plain white flour
½ tsp bicarbonate of soda

tablespoon   fork
wooden spoon   sieve
baking tray   2 mixing bowls

1 Pre-heat the oven at 190°C/375°F/Gas 5.
2 Place the margarine, peanut butter and sugar in a bowl and beat well until light and fluffy, about 5 minutes.

3 Beat in the egg and milk until well mixed. Sift the flour and bicarbonate of soda into a bowl and fold in gently until evenly distributed.
4 Shape the dough into small balls with the hands. Place them, a little apart, onto greased baking trays. Press down with the flat of the hand. Use a fork to make a criss-cross pattern on the top of each cookie.
5 Bake the biscuits in the pre-heated oven for 12–15 minutes until risen and lightly browned. Cool on a wire rack.

Makes 20.   *Cooking time: 12–15 minutes.*

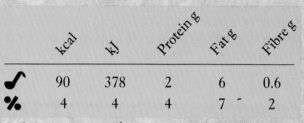

	kcal	kJ	Protein g	Fat g	Fibre g
♪	90	378	2	6	0.6
%	4	4	4	7	2

Don't eat too many!

◆ CHICKEN SATAY WITH PEANUT SAUCE ■

These little kebabs are very popular in Indonesia and the Far East where they are sold from stalls in the street. The longer you can leave the chicken in the marinade the better.

225 g uncooked chicken meat from
2 breast joints
juice of ½ lemon (1½ tbs)
2 tbs soy sauce
1 clove garlic, crushed
1 tsp root ginger, peeled and grated
black pepper

Peanut sauce
2 tbs smooth *or* crunchy peanut butter
50 g creamed coconut dissolved in
4 tbs hot water
1 tbs soy sauce
1 tbs lemon juice
milk
4 cocktail sticks *or* skewers

kitchen knife
tablespoon
teaspoon

lemon squeezer
bowl
saucepan

1 Cut the chicken meat into small pieces and place in a bowl with the lemon juice, soy sauce, garlic, ginger and black pepper.
2 Mix the peanut butter with all the remaining sauce ingredients except the milk. Pour into a saucepan and heat gently. If the sauce starts to thicken too much, thin with milk.
3 Thread the chicken pieces onto skewers or cocktail sticks and cook under a medium grill for about 6–8 minutes, turning from time to time.
4 Serve with the peanut sauce on the side to use as a dip.

Serves 2.   *Cooking time: 6–8 minutes.*

	kcal	kJ	Protein g	Fat g	Fibre g
🍴	372	1555	25	28	1
%	17	17	47	34	4

◆ SESAME FISH FINGERS ■

Here is a tasty homemade variation on bought fish fingers. Serve with tomato sauce.

450 g white fish fillets: coley, huss, cod or haddock
25 g sesame seeds
25 g fresh wholemeal breadcrumbs
salt and pepper
25 g plain flour
1 egg, beaten
oil for greasing

kitchen knife   baking tray
fork

1 Set the oven to 190°C/375°F/Gas 5 and lightly grease a baking tray.
2 Skin the fish if necessary and remove any bones. Cut into chunky fingers.

3 Mix the sesame seeds and breadcrumbs with the seasoning and place in a shallow bowl. Put the flour and egg into two more bowls.
4 Lightly coat each piece of fish first with flour, then with egg and finally with the sesame seed and breadcrumb mixture.
5 Place all the fingers on the prepared tray and baked for 15–20 minutes, depending on the thickness.

Serves 4.   *Cooking time: 15–20 minutes.*

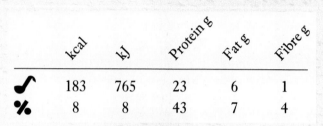

	kcal	kJ	Protein g	Fat g	Fibre g
♪	183	765	23	6	1
%	8	8	43	7	4

◆ SPICED LENTILS OR TARKA DHAL

This is a popular Indian dish. It can be made with any kind of lentils but orange split lentils are the easiest to find in the UK. Lentils provide a cheap source of protein and the dish can be served with Vegetable Curry (page 101) and rice as part of a vegetarian meal.

175 g split orange lentils
700 ml water
1 tsp turmeric
2 tbs polyunsaturated vegetable oil
1–3 dried red chillies
1 tsp whole cumin seeds
1 small onion, peeled and thinly sliced
1 clove garlic, peeled and crushed
salt

teaspoon	plate
wooden spoon	small saucepan with lid
kitchen knife	sieve
measuring jug	small frying pan

1 Tip the lentils onto a plate and pick out any stones or strange items. Wash the lentils in a sieve.
2 Put the lentils in a pan with the water and turmeric and bring to the boil. Cover and simmer for 45–50 minutes, stirring occasionally.
3 Meanwhile prepare the spicy flavourings. The more chillies you use the hotter it will be. Heat the vegetable oil in a small frying pan and fry the whole chillies and cumin seeds for 1 minute.
4 Add the onion and garlic to the pan and continue frying briskly until the onion is well browned. Stir this into the lentils and season with salt. Do not eat the chillies.

Serves 4–6.   *Cooking time: 45–50 minutes.*

CHILLI PEPPERS

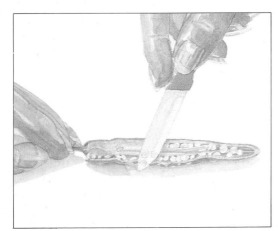

Remove the seeds from fresh or dried chillies to reduce the heat. Always wash your hands after preparing chillies since they irritate the skin.

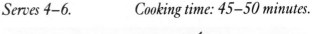
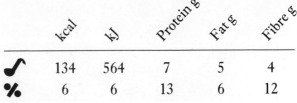

	kcal	kJ	Protein g	Fat g	Fibre g
♪	134	564	7	5	4
%	6	6	13	6	12

◆ MEXICAN TACOS ◆

These crispy corn shells can be served as in the United States with a little minced beef cooked with the taco spices which often come with the shells or you can fill them with these typically Mexican refried beans.

1 clove garlic, peeled and cut in half
½ onion, roughly chopped
1 tbs polyunsaturated cooking oil
1 × 430 g can red kidney beans, well drained
1 small dried red chilli, crushed *or*
1–2 teaspoons ground chilli powder
pepper
8 taco shells
4 lettuce leaves, shredded
50 g Cheddar cheese, grated
chilli sauce

kitchen knife
tablespoon
slotted spoon
wooden spoon

can opener
potato masher
frying pan
baking tray

1 Fry the garlic and onion in very hot oil for a few minutes to flavour it. Remove from the pan with a slotted spoon.
2 Place the beans in the pan and stir and mash for about 10 minutes.
3 Meanwhile set the oven as directed on the pack of taco shells. Place the taco shells on a baking tray and heat through in the oven.
4 Spoon a little of the bean mixture into each taco shell and top with lettuce and grated cheese and chilli sauce.

Serves 4.   *Cooking time: 15 minutes.*

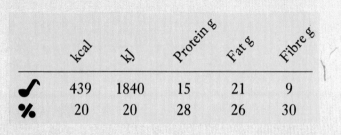

	kcal	kJ	Protein g	Fat g	Fibre g
♩	439	1840	15	21	9
%	20	20	28	26	30

◆ MEAT LOAF ◆

This is a very quick microwave recipe. It uses baked beans to add protein and so cuts down on the amount of minced beef which needs to be used. The egg helps to bind the loaf together.

1 onion, peeled and finely chopped
300 g lean minced beef
1 × 225 g can curried or plain baked beans
50 g fresh wholemeal breadcrumbs
1 egg, beaten
1 tbs tomato purée
½ tsp ground cumin
pepper

bowl
chopping board
wooden spoon
kitchen knife

fork
450 g glass loaf tin or
suitable container
microwave oven

1 Place the onion and meat in a basin and microwave on full power for 3–4 minutes, stirring after every minute. Pour off the fat.
2 Mash the contents of the can of beans with a fork and mix into the meal and onion.
3 Add all the remaining ingredients and mix well together.
4 Spoon the mixture into a 450 g dish and cook on full power for 15 minutes. Leave to stand for 5 minutes. Turn out and cut into slices to serve.

Serves 4. *Cooking time: 18–19 minutes.*

	kcal	kJ	Protein g	Fat g	Fibre g
🥄	262	1092	20	14	5
%	12	12	38	17	18

CEREALS

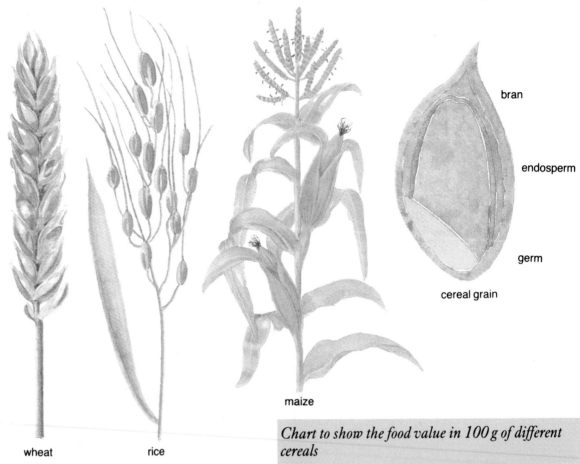

bran

endosperm

germ

cereal grain

maize

wheat   rice

Cereals such as wheat, rice, and maize are plant seeds. They are important foods all over the world. They are cheap to grow and provide a valuable source of **energy** and **dietary fibre**. Whole grain cereals such as brown rice or wholemeal flour contain more dietary fibre than refined cereals such as white rice and flour. Refining takes away the outer husk of seeds – the source of dietary fibre.

Cereals provide us with **protein**. For vegetarians who do not eat animal foods, bread, pasta, and breakfast cereals are useful foods. Cereals contain **starch**, a most important source of **energy**. You can show the presence of starch in food using the **starch test** on page 15.

In Britain we need to increase the amount of cereal foods that we eat, especially whole grain cereals such as wholemeal flour. Each year more and more people are eating wholemeal bread and breakfast cereals.

Chart to show the food value in 100 g of different cereals

cereals	kcal	protein	fat	fibre
cornmeal (maize)	368	9 g	3 g	not available
white rice (raw)	361	6.5 g	1 g	2 g
white wheat flour	337	11 g	1 g	3 g
oatmeal (raw)	401	12 g	9 g	7 g
rye flour (100% extraction)	335	8 g	2 g	not available

Source: McCance and Widdowson

1 Which of the cereals contains the most
  a fibre **b** fat **c** protein?
2 Which cereal do you eat most often? Name three foods made from that cereal.
3 What is meant by 'refined cereals'? What happens if you refine **a** brown rice
  b wholewheat flour?
4 What is the main food value of cereals?
5 How could you increase the amount of cereals that you eat?

52

Finding out about breakfast cereals

[i] Make a collection of different breakfast cereal packets – Cornflakes, Shredded Wheat, Allbran, etc.

An average serving of two Weetabix (37.5 g) provides at least 17 percent of the daily recommended requirements for the average adult of the vitamins listed and iron.

TYPICAL NUTRITIONAL COMPOSITION			
	Per 100 g		Per 100 g
Fat	2.0 g	Dietary Fibre	12.9 g
Protein	10.5 g	Vitamins:	
Available		Niacin	10.0 mg
Carbohydrate	66.8 g	Riboflavin (B$_2$)	1.0 mg
Energy	1400 kJ	Thiamin (B$_1$)	0.7 mg
	335 kcal	Iron	6.0 mg

THIS PACK CONTAINS SIX 2-BISCUIT SERVINGS

A First, look at the Weetabix packet on this page and answer the five questions below. Then answer the same five questions for each breakfast cereal you have collected.

1 Name the breakfast cereal and the cereal it is made from.

Weetabix   –made from whole wheat

2 In 100 g of breakfast cereal what is   **a** the amount of fibre   **b** the energy value in kilocalories or kilojoules?
3 How much would you eat? Look at the average serving.
4 What claims does the food manufacturer make about this breakfast cereal?

B Compare the fibre content of different breakfast cereals. Fill in a chart like the one below, then draw up a bar chart.

Breakfast cereal	amount of fibre in 100g
Weetabix	12·9g

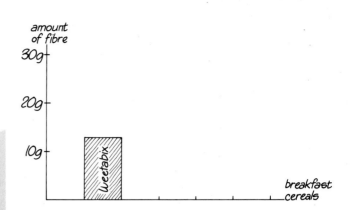
Bar chart to show fibre content

C Compare the energy value of different breakfast cereals. Copy the chart and the bar chart and fill in your results.

Breakfast cereal	energy in kilocalories or kilojoules in 100g
Weetabix	335 kcal

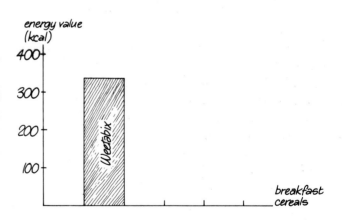
Bar chart to show energy value of breakfast cereals

1 Why do you think the fibre content and energy value of breakfast cereals varies?
2 More and more people are eating breakfast cereals. Why do you think this is?
3 When do people eat breakfast cereals other than at breakfast time? Give examples, and say when you eat them.

Finding out about rice

ⓘ How much does rice weigh when it is cooked?

Work in groups. Each group chooses a type of rice – long grain rice, brown rice, short grain rice, basmati rice, easy-cook rice, etc.

You need:

large saucepan	sieve
measuring jug	plate
scales	large bowl

1 Measure enough water to half fill the saucepan. Bring to the boil.
2 Add 100 g of rice, return to the boil, and cook until soft (see packet instructions).
3 Strain the cooked rice through a sieve held over a large bowl.
4 Weigh the rice and put on a plate. Measure the strained water.
5 Copy the chart below and fill in your results. Weigh out the amount of rice you would eat.
6 Collect the information from the other groups and complete the chart.
7 When you have tasted the rice, clear away and test the strained water for starch using the iodine test (see page 15).

type of rice	white, long	brown rice
weight before cooking	100g	
weight after cooking	240g	
look and taste	long white grains- crunchy and nice	
how much would you eat?	120g	
water added		
strained water		

Why is the cooked rice heavier than the raw rice? Which type of rice did you like best? Which would you eat the most of?
Choose your favourite rice dish using one of these rices, and plan a complete evening meal.

Composition of rice

	raw brown	cooked brown	raw white	cooked white
energy	360 kcal	119 kcal	363 kcal	109 kcal
water	12 g	70 g	12 g	72 g
protein	7.5 g	2.5 g	6.7 g	2 g
fat	1.9 g	0.6 g	0.4 g	0.1 g
carbo- hydrate	77.4 g	25.5 g	80.4 g	24.2 g
fibre	0.9 g	0.3 g	0.3 g	0.1 g
calcium	32 mg	12 mg	24 mg	10 mg
sodium	9 mg	282 mg*	5 mg	374 mg*

*The amount of sodium in cooked rice depends upon the amount of salt added to the water.

Source: US Rice Council

Ⓠ 1 Why has the amount of water in raw and cooked rice changed?
2 Which cooked rice has the most a protein b fat c fibre d the highest energy value?
3 Do you think rice is a good source of dietary fibre? Show the amount of fibre in four other foods as part of your answer.
4 Using the charts on this page, work out the food value for the amount of rice that *you* would eat in a meal.

For example, you may eat 120 g of white rice.

Food value of 120 g of cooked white rice:

energy		fat	
water	84 g	carbohydrate	
protein		fibre	

How to do it?
100 g of cooked white rice contains roughly 70 g water, so how much water is there in 120 g of rice?
1 g of rice contains $^{70}/_{100} = 0.7$ g water
120 g rice contains $0.7 \times 120 = 84$ g water

In the same way work out the amount of energy, protein, fat, carbohydrate, and fibre.
5 Which is healthier, brown or white rice? In your answer, remember how much you would like to eat of each rice.

Muesli

1 Make up the muesli for every group member in a large bowl, then share into small bowls.
2 Mix together the flaked cereals, bran, wheatgerm or oatmeal. Use up to 20–25 g per person.
3 Add enough milk to soak the cereals, then leave to stand.
4 Chop up the dates or figs and add the dried fruits to the mixture. Remember, you are not adding sugar to this recipe, so use enough fruit for sweetness. Mix in the seeds of your choice.
5 Grate or chop the fresh fruit finely, mix with lemon juice to prevent browning, then add to the muesli.
6 Taste the mixture and change your recipe if necessary.
7 Spoon into small bowls.

Dr Bircher-Benner invented a recipe for muesli and served it to patients in his Swiss Clinic as part of a healthy eating plan. The original dish contained oatmeal, cream, honey, grated apple, and chopped nuts. Over the years recipes for muesli have changed and we now use more cereal foods and less fresh fruit than the original recipe.

[i] Invent your own muesli recipe

Work in groups. Weigh out a quantity of each ingredient that you choose. At the end, write out the exact amounts used in your invented recipe.

Choose from the following:

Cereals Flaked cereals – oat flakes, wheat flakes, barley flakes, rye flakes, bran, wheatgerm, oatmeal

Dried fruits and seeds Currants, sultanas, dates, figs, sesame seeds, sunflower seeds

Fresh fruits Apples or pears with a little lemon juice

Some milk

You need:
scales
large bowl
small bowl
tablespoon
chopping board

knife
grater
bowl and spoon for each person

Finding out about cereals

[Q] 1 Copy the chart and fill in each section using the cereals you chose for your muesli recipe.

cereal food	size (draw, measure, or stick in an example)	colour	texture and taste
rye flakes	⬭ 9mm × 5mm	brown and cream	crunchy, crisp, nutty
wheatgerm			

2 Use the food packets or food tables to find the nutritional value of 100 g of each cereal food.
3 In the muesli recipe, what do you think is the importance of **a** the cereal foods **b** the dried fruits and seeds **c** the fresh fruit **d** the milk?
4 Was Dr Bircher-Benner right to choose muesli as a healthy food? Give your reasons.
5 Compare the ingredients of packet muesli with your own recipe. Which do you prefer and why?
6 Invent a healthy breakfast food that you think people of your age would like. Make a list of the ingredients that you would choose.

◆ CORN CHOWDER ◆

Chowder is the American name for a soup thick with vegetables and potatoes and usually made with milk. It is often substantial enough to form the main course of a meal.

1 onion, finely chopped
2 potatoes, peeled and diced (approx 350 g)
450 ml chicken or fish stock
450 ml skimmed milk
pepper
150 g frozen sweetcorn kernels or
small tin sweetcorn
75 g frozen peas

Optional extras:
100 g smoked fish fillet, skinned
or
½ small cauliflower cut into florets

kitchen knife
chopping board
potato peeler
wooden spoon

large saucepan with lid
measuring jug

1 Place the onions, potatoes, stock, milk and seasoning in a saucepan and bring to the boil.
2 Reduce the heat cover and simmer for 15 minutes.
3 Add the sweetcorn and peas and bring to the boil. Simmer for a further 10 minutes.

NB If using optional extras add at the beginning of the cooking time.

Serves 4.   *Cooking time: 25 minutes.*

	kcal	kJ	Protein g	Fat g	Fibre g
♪	207	869	14	1	4
%	10	10	27	1	15

Good source of calcium

■ BROWN RICE SALAD ■

Brown rice gives this salad a chewy texture.

150 g cold cooked brown rice (approx 60 g raw)
1 × 200 g can mexicorn, drained
1 tbs freshly chopped parsley
1 tbs salad oil, polyunsaturated *or* olive
1 tsp cider vinegar
salt and pepper

kitchen knife   teaspoon
chopping board   mixing bowl
tablespoon

Place all the ingredients in a large bowl and toss well together.

Serves 4.

	kcal	kJ	Protein g	Fat g	Fibre g
🥄	141	589	3	5	2
%	6.5	6.5	5	6	7

■ WHITE RICE SALAD ■

Cold cooked rice can be used as the base for all sorts of salads. This one uses fruits in a savoury way.

200 g cold cooked rice
½ green pepper, seeded and
finely chopped (50 g)
1 red skinned eating apple,
cored and chopped (50 g)
1½ tbs peanuts (50 g)
1 tbs raisins (25 g)
salt and freshly ground pepper
2 tbs salad oil, polyunsaturated *or* olive
2 tsp lemon juice *or* cider vinegar

kitchen knife   mixing bowl
tablespoon   chopping board
teaspoon

Place all the ingredients in a large bowl and toss well together.

Serves 4.

	kcal	kJ	Protein g	Fat g	Fibre g
🥄	190	801	3	11	2
%	9	9	6	14	6

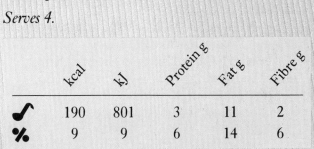

MILLET PILAF

Serve instead of rice with kebabs and casseroles.

1 onion, very finely chopped
1 tbs polyunsaturated oil
250 g whole millet
1 vegetable stock cube dissolved
in 650 ml boiling water
salt and black pepper
Optional flavourings
1 tsp ground cinnamon
1 tbs flaked almonds
1 tbs raisins

kitchen knife	chopping board
teaspoon	wooden spoon
tablespoon	measuring jug
saucepan with lid	fork

1 Fry the onion in the oil for 3–4 minutes. Add the millet and continue frying for a further minute.
2 Pour on the vegetable stock and add seasoning and any flavourings to be used.
3 Cover with a lid and bring to the boil. Stir millet and turn the heat as low as it will go.
4 Simmer for about 30 minutes until all the liquid has been absorbed and the millet is soft and fluffy.

Serves 4.   *Cooking time: 35 minutes.*

	kcal	kJ	Protein g	Fat g	Fibre g
🥄	291	1216	4	6	1
%	14	14	8	7	3

◆ NOODLES WITH PEAS AND HAM ◆

Any kind of noodles can be used to make this dish. Experiment with Chinese dried noodles, Italian green or spinach spaghetti or tagliatelle, buckwheat noodles or Chinese rice or bean noodles.

1 tbs flaked almonds or desiccated coconut
2 tbs polyunsaturated cooking oil
100 g frozen peas
100 g cooked ham, cut into thin strips
1 tsp soy sauce
grated rind and juice of 1 orange
250 g noodles, cooked as directed on the packet

| grater | wok or deep frying |
| tablespoon | pan |

1 Toast the almonds or coconut under a grill to lightly brown them. Keep on one side.
2 Heat the cooking oil in a wok or deep frying pan and stir fry the peas for 1 minute.
3 Add the ham, soy sauce, grated orange and juice and the noodles and toss over a high heat until all the liquid has evaporated.

Serves 4.   *Cooking time: 2–3 minutes.*

	kcal	kJ	Protein g	Fat g	Fibre g
🥄	366	1524	15	10	5
%	17	17	28	11	18

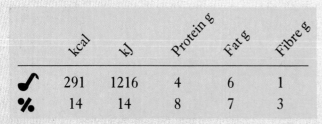

◆ PASTA POMODORO ◼

A good tomato sauce is all that is needed to turn a bowl of pasta into a good meal. Serve with a green salad and a good sprinkling of grated Parmesan cheese.

1 × 400 g can tomatoes
1 carrot, peeled and grated
½ small onion, chopped
1 tsp tomato puree
salt and pepper
500 g fresh pasta or 250 g dried pasta
(spaghetti, tagliatelle or shapes)
1 tbs olive oil

kitchen knife   chopping board
grater   small saucepan
teaspoon   large saucepan

1 Place the contents of the can of tomatoes in a small saucepan with the carrot, onion, tomato puree and seasoning.
2 Bring to the boil and simmer for 20 minutes. Use this sauce as it is or purée in a blender or processor.
3 Cook the fresh pasta for 3–4 minutes or the dried pasta as directed on the pack. Plunge into a large pan of boiling water.
4 Test the pasta is just tender to the bite (al dente).
5 Drain well and then toss in olive oil. Spoon onto serving plates and top with the tomato sauce.

Serves 4.   *Cooking time: 20 minutes.*

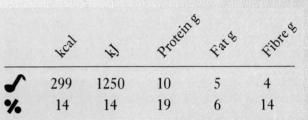

	kcal	kJ	Protein g	Fat g	Fibre g
🎵	299	1250	10	5	4
%	14	14	19	6	14

◆ BROWN RICE KEDGEREE ■

This is an Anglo-Indian dish which was very popular for breakfast in Victorian times. Today it can be served at any meal.

200 g cooked brown rice (dried weight 80 g)
200 g smoked mackerel fillets, skinned, boned and flaked
2 hard boiled eggs, chopped coarsely
150 ml soured cream *or* yoghurt
salt and black pepper
25 g butter
3 tbs freshly chopped parsley

kitchen knife
tablespoon
chopping board

mixing bowl
casserole or pie dish
fork

1 Set the oven to 190°C/375°F/Gas 5 and grease a casserole or pie dish.
2 Mix the brown rice with the smoked fish, eggs, soured cream and seasoning.
3 Spoon into the prepared casserole dish and dot with butter. Bake for 20–25 minutes. Serve each portion with a generous sprinkling of chopped parsley.

Serves 4.   *Cooking time: 20–25 minutes.*

	kcal	kJ	Protein g	Fat g	Fibre g
🎵	332	1385	21	18	0.1
%	15	15	40	21	0.3

HONEY CRISPIES

CHOCOLATE TRUFFLES

Almost any kind of dry breakfast cereal can be used in this recipe. Add a spoonful of raisins or chopped nuts for a new flavour.

20 g cornflakes
20 g rice crispies
20 g bran flakes
50 g sugar
1 tbs runny honey
15 g margarine

tablespoon
wooden spoon
paper cake cases

mixing bowl
small saucepan

1 Mix the dry ingredients in a bowl.
2 Heat the sugar and honey in a saucepan. Bring to the boil and simmer gently for 5 minutes.
3 Stir in the margarine and pour over the dry ingredients and mix together.
4 Working quickly before the mixture hardens, spoon clusters into cake cases.
Note: This boiled mixture becomes extremely hot. Do not touch it with your hands or eat the crispies until they are cold.

Makes 12.   *Cooking time: 5 minutes.*

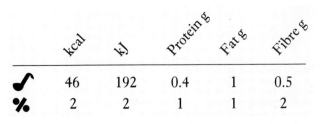

	kcal	kJ	Protein g	Fat g	Fibre g
♪	46	192	0.4	1	0.5
%	2	2	1	1	2

Breakfast cereals make a good high-fibre base for these delicious sweets.

25 g firm margarine
1 tbs milk
15 g sugar
100 g plain chocolate
50 g rolled oats
2 Weetabix, crushed
50 g raisins

tablespoon
teaspoon
wooden spoon

paper sweet cases
saucepan

1 Melt the margarine, with sugar and chocolate in a saucepan.
2 Stir in all the dry ingredients and mix with the milk until stiff.
3 Drop teaspoonfuls into small paper cases and place in the fridge to set.

Makes 26.   *Cooking time: about 1–2 minutes.*

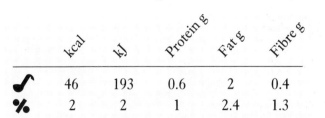

	kcal	kJ	Protein g	Fat g	Fibre g
♪	46	193	0.6	2	0.4
%	2	2	1	2.4	1.3

Good source of iron

■ FLAPJACK ■

Traditionally made with rolled oats, these crunchy fingers can be made with a variety of other flaked cereals. Try a mixture of oats, millet and rice or any two of these.

100 g firm margarine
50 g demerara sugar
1 tbs syrup
75 g rolled oats
50 g flaked millet
50 g flaked rice

tablespoon   18 cm square baking tin
wooden spoon   saucepan

1 Set the oven to 180°C/350°F/Gas 4 and line an 18 cm square baking tray with greased baking paper.
2 Melt the margarine, sugar and syrup in a pan and then stir in all the dry ingredients.
3 Pack the mixture into the baking tray and press well down and into the corners.
4 Bake for 20–25 minutes until golden. Mark into squares. Leave to cool in the tin and then break into squares along the marked lines.

Makes 9 squares.   *Cooking time: 20–25 minutes.*

	kcal	kJ	Protein g	Fat g	Fibre g
✓	180	754	2	10	1
%	8	8	3	11	4

■ OATMEAL SCONES ■

The addition of 25 g grated Cheddar cheese makes a delicious variation to this well-textured scone.

100 g medium oatmeal
150 ml skimmed milk
150 g self raising flour
1 tsp baking powder
½ tsp salt

teaspoon   baking tray
mixing bowl   rolling pin
scone or biscuit cutter   wire rack

1 Soak the oatmeal in the milk in a large bowl and leave to stand for 30 minutes.
2 Set the oven to 180°C/350°F/Gas 4. Grease the baking tray.
3 Sift the remaining dry ingredients into the bowl and mix to a soft dough.
4 Turn onto a floured board and knead lightly for 2 minutes.
5 Roll out to about 1½ cm thick and cut into 6 scones. Place on the prepared baking tray and bake for 20 minutes. Cool on a wire rack.

Makes 6.   *Cooking time: 20 minutes.*

	kcal	kJ	Protein g	Fat g	Fibre g
✓	160	668	6	2	2
%	7	7	11	2	7

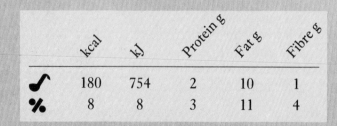
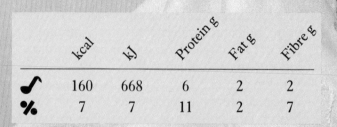

◆ SODA BREAD ■

Mixing wholemeal and white flour results in a lighter, less crumbly loaf. For a change of flavour make the bread with 2 tablespoons of very finely chopped celery and half a teaspoon of mixed dried herbs.

350 g wholemeal flour
100 g plain white flour
1 level tsp salt
2 level tsp cream of tartar
1 level tsp bicarbonate of soda
25 g hard margarine
300 ml buttermilk, or skimmed milk

teaspoons   large mixing bowl
kitchen knife   measuring jug
pastry brush   baking tray

1 Set the oven to 200°C/400°F/Gas 6 and lightly flour a baking tray. Mix the flours with the cream of tartar and bicarbonate of soda.
2 Rub in the margarine until the mixture looks like fine breadcrumbs. Add the herbs and celery if using.
3 Pour on the milk and mix to a soft dough.
4 Turn onto a floured board and knead gently for 6–8 minutes until the dough is smooth and there are no cracks in it.
5 Shape into a 20 cm round and flatten slightly. Slash a cross on the top with a knife and place on the floured tray. Brush the top with a little more milk and bake for 40 minutes.

Makes 1 loaf – serves 10.   Cooking time: 40 minutes.

	kcal	kJ	Protein g	Fat g	Fibre g
♪	174	730	6.7	3	4
%	8	8	13	3	13

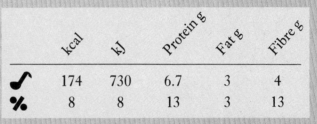

◆ CHICKEN BURGERS

Serve with sesame buns lined with lettuce leaves and your favourite relish.

50 g fresh wholemeal breadcrumbs
or
30 g cracked wheat or bulgar
or
30 g oatmeal
4 chicken thighs (approx 280 g meat) skinned and
minced or finely chopped
50 g mushrooms very finely chopped
½ tsp Worcestershire sauce
pinch dried tarragon
salt and pepper
a little oil for frying
wholemeal flour for rolling out

fish slice   basin
kitchen knife   mixing bowl
teaspoon   frying pan
fork

1 If you have chosen to use cracked wheat or oatmeal, cover it with cold water and leave to stand for 15 minutes. Drain and squeeze dry.
2 Place your chosen cereal ingredient in a mixing bowl and add all the remaining ingredients.
3 Flour the work surface and shape the mixture into a roll. Cut into four pieces and shape into burgers. Fry in a very little oil on each side for 6–7 minutes. Alternatively brush with a little oil and cook under the grill.

Serves 2.   *Cooking time: 12–14 minutes.*

	kcal	kJ	Protein g	Fat g	Fibre g
🍴	448	1871	28	33	3
%	21	21	52	40	10

◆ RYE AND RAISIN TEABREAD ■

Rye flours give a very dark appearance and almost nutty taste to bread and cakes.

150 g wholemeal flour
100 g rye flour
100 g raisins
50 g no-soak prunes, stoned and chopped
100 ml milk
1 egg beaten
2 tbs black treacle or molasses

tablespoon · mixing bowl
fork · kitchen knife
wooden spoon · measuring jug
450 g loaf tin · saucepan

1 Set the oven to 100°C/325°F/Gas 3 and grease a 450 g loaf tin.
2 Mix the two flours, raisins and chopped prunes in a bowl.
3 Heat the molasses and milk together until the molasses dissolves. Remove from the heat, beat in the egg and pour over the dry ingredients.
4 Spoon the mixture into the prepared tin and smooth over the top. Bake for 1 hour.

Makes 1 × 450 g loaf.   *Cooking time: 1 hour.*
Serves 10.

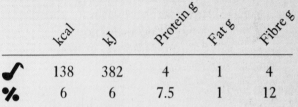

	kcal	kJ	Protein g	Fat g	Fibre g
🥄	138	382	4	1	4
%	6	6	7.5	1	12

Good source of iron ·

◆ SPEEDY SAUSAGE PIZZA ◆

This recipe makes a large pizza which can be cut into squares. However the pizza dough can be broken into pieces and rolled out to make four individual pizza bases.

200 g brown *or* wholemeal flour
7 g fast-acting yeast
15 g polyunsaturated lard *or* firm margarine
5 fl oz hand hot water
Topping
1 tbs vegetable oil
2 tbs tomato purée
200 g tomatoes, thinly sliced
2 Frankfurter sausages, thinly sliced
1 tsp dried oregano
150 g Gouda cheese, grated

kitchen knife   measuring jug
teaspoon   pastry brush
33 cm × 18 cm baking tray   polythene bag
mixing bowl   small bowl

1 Set the oven to 220°C/425°F/Gas 7 and grease the baking tray.
2 Place the flour, salt and yeast in a bowl and rub in the fat.
3 Pour on the water and mix to a stiff dough. Turn out on to a floured surface and knead for 3–4 minutes.
4 Place in an oiled polythene bag and leave in a warm place for 10 minutes.
5 On a lightly floured surface, roll out the dough and use to line the prepared baking tray making a lip around the edge.
6 Mix the oil and tomato purée and brush all over the top of the pizza base.
7 Cover with tomato, sausage, oregano and cheese and bake for about 30 minutes.

Serves 4.   *Cooking time: 30 minutes.*

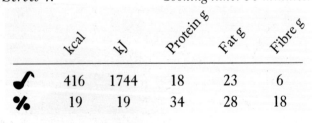

	kcal	kJ	Protein g	Fat g	Fibre g
♪	416	1744	18	23	6
%	19	19	34	28	18

◆ OATMEAL AND APPLE CRUNCH BARS

If you have a sweet tooth, sprinkle the top of the bars with a little demerara sugar just before cooking. For a change, add half a teaspoon of ground ginger to the base and topping mixture.

300 g cooking apples, peeled and sliced
50 g raisins
rind and juice of half a medium sized orange
1½ tbs water
150 g wholemeal flour
100 g medium oatmeal
100 g margarine
50 g light muscovado or brown sugar
a little demerara sugar for sprinkling on top, if desired

kitchen knife   baking tin
tablespoon   chopping board
small pan with lid   bowl

1 Set oven to 190°C/375°F/Gas 5.
2 Place the apples in a pan with the raisins, orange rind and juice and water. Cover and simmer for 8–10 minutes until pulpy. Leave to cool.
3 Place the flour and oatmeal in a bowl.
4 Add the margarine cut into small pieces. Rub the fat into the dry ingredients until the mixture resembles fine breadcrumbs.
5 Stir in the sugar.
6 Sprinkle half this mixture over the base of a 18 cm square greased tin.
7 Press down lightly and spread with the apple mixture. Cover with remaining dry ingredients. Sprinkle with sugar if using. Bake for 35 minutes until lightly browned.
8 Leave to cool in the tin. Cut into 8 bars to serve.

Makes 8 bars.   *Cooking time: 35 minutes.*

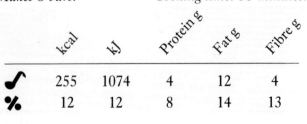

	kcal	kJ	Protein g	Fat g	Fibre g
♪	255	1074	4	12	4
%	12	12	8	14	13

◆ HOT CROSS BUNS

These Easter favourites seem to taste even better when made with wholemeal flour. Use more raisins if you do not have any candied peel.

250 g wholemeal flour
1 sachet (15 g) fast acting yeast
¼ tsp each: cinnamon, nutmeg, mixed spices
25 g light Muscovado *or* brown sugar
½ tsp salt
50 g raisins *or* currants
25 g chopped candied peel
75 ml lukewarm skimmed milk
75 ml lukewarm water
1 egg, beaten
25 g butter, melted

teaspoon
wooden spoon
mixing bowl
measuring jug
fork

small saucepan
baking sheet
pastry brush
greased paper

1 Place all the dry ingredients in a large bowl and mix well together.

2 Make a well in the centre of the dry ingredients. Mix the milk and water, with half the beaten egg and the melted butter and pour into the well. Blend to a smooth dough.
3 Turn onto a floured surface and knead for 8–10 minutes until smooth and elastic.
4 Divide into 6 equal pieces and shape into balls. Place on a floured baking sheet and press down a little. Cover with greased paper and put to rise in a warm place until double in size. This takes about one hour.
5 Brush with the remaining beaten egg and then cut a cross in the top of each bun.
6 Bake at 200°C/400°F/Gas 6 for 25 minutes until golden brown.

Makes 6.   *Cooking time: 25 minutes.*

	kcal	kJ	Protein g	Fat g	Fibre g
🥄	231	969	7	5	5
%	11	11	13	7	16

FINNISH FRUIT PLAIT

This sweet bread is known as Pulla in Finland and is eaten at the weekend and on feast days and holidays.

250 g plain white flour
15 g fast acting yeast (sachet)
¼ tsp salt
25 g raisins
35 g dates, chopped
25 g sugar
125 ml lukewarm skimmed milk
50 g margarine, melted
1 egg, beaten

kitchen knife
teaspoon
tablespoon
sieve
fork

pastry brush
mixing bowl
measuring jug
baking tray

1 Sift the flour into a large mixing bowl and stir in the raisins, dates, yeast and salt.
2 Stir the sugar into the milk in a measuring jug and continue stirring until all the sugar has dissolved.
3 Make a well in the centre of the flour mixture and pour in the milk. Add the margarine and half the beaten egg.
4 Mix to a smooth dough with your hands and knead lightly for 3–4 minutes. Leave to stand for 20 minutes.
5 With floured hands divide the mixture into three portions and roll each portion into a sausage shape about 35 cm long and 3 cm across
6 Plait the rolls of dough and place on a floured baking tray. Leave to stand for a further 20 minutes.
7 Set the oven to 220°C/425°F/Gas 7 and brush the top of the loaf with the remaining beaten egg and bake for 10–12 minutes. Then lower the heat to 190°C/375°F/Gas 5 and bake for another 15 minutes.

Makes 1 loaf – serves 10.
Cooking time: 20–25 minutes.

	kcal	kJ	Protein g	Fat g	Fibre g
♩	158	661	4	5	1.5
%	7	7	8	6	5

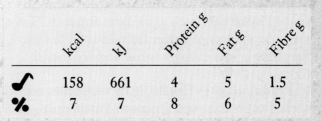

LEAFY VEGETABLES

What is a leafy vegetable?

cabbage   lettuce   spinach

Leafy vegetables such as cabbage, spinach, and lettuce grow above the ground, whereas root vegetables such as carrots grow under the soil. Leafy vegetables are important in a healthy diet as they provide us with **dietary fibre**, **vitamin C**, and **minerals** such as calcium and iron. Since they contain lots of **water** (lettuce is 96% water), they have a **low energy value** and are useful foods for slimmers.

Traditionally in Britain, leafy vegetables are served as an accompaniment to a main meal. In many other countries, leafy vegetables are cooked with other ingredients and served as the main dish – for example, stuffed cabbage leaves.

Green and yellow vegetables add colour to meals. Crunchy stems such as celery and raw vegetables such as cabbage add a variety of textures.

Vegetables are plants. The leafy vegetables we eat are different parts of different plants. Watercress is the whole plant, including the stem; spinach is eaten for its leaves, although in some countries the stems are cooked; and we eat the flower of cauliflowers.

The table below shows some of the vegetables divided into different groups. Some leafy vegetables belong to two or more groups. You may disagree with the examples in the table. For example, if you eat the leaves of celery then this vegetable fits into several groups.

Part of the plant that is eaten

the whole plant above ground	asparagus	mung beansprouts	
stems	celery	rhubarb	fennel
leaves	chicory	lettuce	spinach
buds and flowers	cauliflower	broccoli	brussels sprouts

Fit these vegetables into the groups shown on the chart:
watercress, parsley, kale, Chinese leaves, cabbage, spring greens, bamboo shoots, calabrese, mustard and cress, chives
Use other books to help you. Add more examples of your own.

Q 1 Give two examples of main meals served with leafy vegetables.
2 Name as many crunchy leafy vegetables as possible.
3 What is the difference between root and leafy vegetables?

Food value chart

food (100 g)	kcal	protein	fat	water	calcium	iron	VitA	VitC	fibre
raw winter cabbage	20	3 g	—	88 g	60 mg	0.6 mg	50 μg	60 mg	3 g
boiled winter cabbage	15	1.7 g	—	93 g	40 mg	0.4 mg	50 μg	20 mg	2 g
lettuce	10	1 g	—	96 g	25 mg	0.9 mg	200 μg	15 mg	1.5 g
watercress	14	3 g	—	91 g	220 mg	1.6 mg	500 μg	60 mg	3 g
parsley	20	5 g	—	79 g	330 mg	8 mg	1500 μg	150 mg	9.1 g
boiled spinach	30	5 g	—	85 g	600 mg	4 mg	1000 μg	25 mg	6 g
brussels sprouts	20	3 g	—	92 g	25 mg	0.5 mg	60 μg	40 mg	3 g
wholemeal bread	220	8.8 g	2.7 g	40 g	25 mg	2.5 mg	—	—	9 g
Cheddar cheese	400	26 g	34 g	37 g	800 mg	0.4 mg	400 μg	—	—

Source: Bender and Bender

Q When you answer these questions, use some of the details from the chart.
1 Why do health experts suggest we try to eat more raw instead of boiled vegetables? Use the details for 'winter cabbage' in your answer.
2 Which two vegetables contain the most
a) water b) calcium c) vitamin C?
3 Which three vegetables would be useful in your diet? Remember, the amount that you like to eat matters.
4 Why do you think lots of slimming diets include leafy vegetables?
5 Look at the food value for lettuce, bread, and cheese. Is a cheese and lettuce sandwich a healthy food? Give your reasons.

The Natural Way To Good Health

Vegetables and their vitamins

1 Old battered vegetables contain little vitamin C, so choose fresh, firm vegetables.

2 Vitamin C is lost when vegetables are chopped up. Prepare vegetables when you need them.

3 Don't leave vegetables to stand in water, as vitamin C and B group vitamins dissolve out and are lost; and don't cook vegetables in lots of water – the vitamins are lost into the cooking water.

4 Don't keep vegetables warm for too long after cooking. Warmth and time destroy vitamin C.

How does water travel round a plant?

2 Add the stick of celery and leave for an hour or longer.

3 Repeat this experiment using cauliflower florets in smaller glasses.

4 Cut up the celery and cauliflower. Draw a diagram to show how the red colouring has spread around the plant. Which parts are coloured most?

Why is the colouring only in certain parts of the plant?
Food and water is carried to plant cells by tubes or 'vascular bundles' which run along the stems of plants. As the food colouring travels up the stem it stains these tubes red.

What can you do with limp vegetables?
Limp vegetables can sometimes be revived by standing them in water. Try this yourself with stalks of parsley, a spinach leaf and stem, or a limp lettuce. Remember that the vitamins which dissolve in water (C and B group) will leak out. However, a crisp vegetable is more pleasant to eat than a soft, wilted leaf.

[e] Trace the route of red food colouring round a plant.

You need:
tall and small glasses
red food colouring
sticks of celery or cauliflower florets
knife

1 Half fill a glass with cold water and mix in 2–3 teaspoons of red colouring.

Find out how green leafy vegetables change during cooking

Green leafy vegetables are often spoiled by overcooking. Some vitamins are lost in the cooking water and the appearance of the vegetable changes.

Work in four groups.

Each group needs:

50 g spinach or other green leafy vegetables
saucepan

white plate
stop watch or timer
slotted spoon or sieve

1 Each group must choose one of the following cooking times: a) 30 seconds b) 1 minute c) 5 minutes d) 10 minutes.
2 Pour 150 ml water into each saucepan and bring to the boil.
3 Keep one leaf of spinach as a control and put the rest in the pan. Time the cooking exactly. Drain each sample as soon as it is ready and place on the plate.
4 Draw a chart like the one below. Taste each sample and compare flavours, colour, and texture with the other groups' cooked spinach. Taste the raw leaf too.

Q 1 How did the spinach change in colour and texture as it cooked?
2 Which cooking method do you like best and why?

Why does the colour change?

Green vegetables contain a plant pigment called chlorophyll. During the first seconds of cooking the colour brightens. The colour becomes dull with longer cooking due to loss of the mineral magnesium, and the release of acid.

Adding sodium bicarbonate to leafy vegetables

In the past, British cooks added a pinch of sodium bicarbonate to the cooking water to brighten green vegetables. They didn't realise that this chemical destroys some of the vitamin C and B group vitamins. The vegetables also became mushy.

Try this out for yourself. Repeat the previous experiment, using 50 g spinach. Cook the spinach by your favourite method, adding 1 level teaspoon of sodium bicarbonate to the cooking water.

How did the colour of the spinach compare with the other results?

	taste	colour	texture
raw leaf spinach			
spinach cooked for 30 seconds			
spinach cooked for 1 minute			
spinach cooked for 5 minutes			
spinach cooked for 10 minutes			

◆ WATERCRESS SOUP ■

This light summer soup can be served hot or cold.

2 bunches watercress, washed and chopped
1 potato (225 g), peeled and chopped
300 ml chicken stock made with a chicken stock cube and boiling water
300 ml skimmed milk
freshly ground black pepper
salt

kitchen knife
teaspoon
wooden spoon

measuring jug
saucepan with lid
cup

1 Place the watercress and potato in a pan with the chicken stock, skimmed milk and black pepper. Cover and bring to the boil. Reduce the heat and simmer for 15 minutes.
2 Rub the soup through a sieve or puree in a food processor or blender.
3 Reheat and serve.

Serves 4.   *Cooking time: 35 minutes.*

	kcal	kJ	Protein g	Fat g	Fibre g
🎵	90	370	4	0.1	1.8
%	4	4	8	0.1	6

◆ THICK CELERY SOUP ◆

This soup can be made without frying the vegetables but this process does bring out the flavour of the vegetables and improves the taste of the soup.

1 tbs polyunsaturated oil
1 onion, (200 g) peeled and sliced
1 head celery (500 g)
2 tbs medium ground oatmeal
800 ml water
1 vegetable *or* chicken stock cube
¼ tsp dried mixed herbs
freshly ground black pepper

wooden spoon
measuring jug
tablespoon
kitchen knife

non-stick saucepan
with lid
sieve, blender or
food processor

1 Heat the vegetable oil in a pan and fry the onion until lightly browned.
2 Add the celery and fry for a further 2–3 minutes.
3 Stir in the oatmeal and then the water, stock cube, herbs and pepper.
4 Bring to the boil and simmer for 20 minutes until the celery is tender.
5 Rub the soup through a sieve or blend in a food processor or blender. Return to the pan and reheat.

Serves 4.   *Cooking time: 20–25 minutes.*

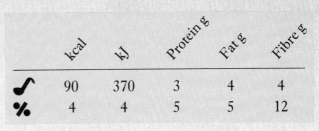

	kcal	kJ	Protein g	Fat g	Fibre g
🥄	90	370	3	4	4
%	4	4	5	5	12

SOUP GARNISHES

Bowls of soup look much more attractive if they are garnished. Use freshly chopped herbs, sprigs of watercress, parsley or dill, or bread croutons prepared in the same way as the croutons in the Spinach Salad (see page 77).

◆ WINTER SALAD ■

Winter salad leaves to go with this recipe might include lettuce, watercress or Chinese Cabbage.

1 large carrot, peeled and grated
juice of ½ lemon
150 g brussels sprouts, very finely chopped
1 tbs raw peanuts, toasted under the grill
1 tbs raisins
1 tbs parsley, freshly chopped
a little grated orange rind
2 tbs plain yoghurt
mixed winter salad leaves

kitchen knife   bowl
tablespoon   lemon squeezer
grater   grill pan

1 Mix the freshly grated carrot with the lemon juice to prevent the carrot from discolouring or drying up.
2 Stir in all the remaining ingredients as they are prepared and toss well together. Serve on a bed of salad leaves in season.

Serves 2.

	kcal	kJ	Protein g	Fat g	Fibre g
♩	161	671	10	7	9
%	8	8	18	8	29

Good source of vitamin C

SPINACH SALAD WITH CRUNCHY CROUTONS

Fresh young spinach leaves are best for this salad. However, if the leaves are very large, cut out the centre rib which may be tough and stringy.

2 cloves garlic, crushed
1 tbs sunflower seed oil
2 thick slices bread
175 g spinach leaves, washed and drained

Dressing

2 tbs olive *or* sunflower seed oil
½ tbs wine *or* cider vinegar
¼ tsp made mustard
salt and freshly ground black pepper

kitchen knife   pastry brush
tablespoon   baking tray
teaspoon   bowl

1 Set the oven to 230°C/450°F/Gas 8.
2 Mix the garlic with the oil and, using the pastry brush, lightly coat the slices of bread.
3 Place on a baking tray and bake for 10 minutes until crisp and brown. Turn once during the cooking time. Remove from the oven and leave to cool.
4 Cut into cubes and keep on one side.
5 Put the spinach leaves into a bowl, tearing any large leaves into smaller pieces. Add the bread croutons.
6 Put the dressing ingredients in a jam jar and screw the lid on. Shake well and pour over the salad before the dressing separates.

Serves 4.   *Cooking time: 10 minutes.*

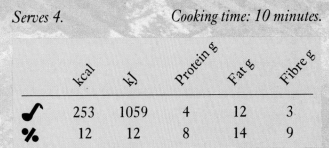

	kcal	kJ	Protein g	Fat g	Fibre g
♪	253	1059	4	12	3
%	12	12	8	14	9

Good source of iron and vitamin C

◆ PICKLED RED CABBAGE

For long lasting pickles the red cabbage should be salted to remove some of the excess water. This takes twenty-four hours. However, quick pickles can be made in the following way. They will keep for a couple of months or so.

350 ml malt vinegar
½ tsp each of grated root ginger, cloves, peppercorns and mustard seed
½ cinnamon stick
1 tbs dark Muscovado *or* brown sugar
¼ large red cabbage (350 g)
½ small onion, finely sliced

saucepan   kitchen knife
tablespoon   jam jars with
teaspoon   vinegar-proof lids

1 Heat the vinegar in pan until just below boiling point. Remove from the heat and add all the spices and sugar. Leave to stand while you prepare the cabbage.

2 Shred the cabbage finely and mix with the onion. Pack into 450 g jam jars with vinegar-proof lids.

3 Strain the vinegar through muslin or a fine strainer and use to fill up the jam jars. Screw down the lids and leave to stand for 2 weeks before using.

Makes 2 jars.   *Cooking time: 1–2 minutes.*

	kcal	kJ	Protein g	Fat g	Fibre g
♪	15	63	0.9	—	1
%	0.7	0.7	2	0	4

◆ ALOO GOBI

The combination of cauliflower and potatoes is a popular one in Northern India and many families have their own recipes which are handed down from generation to generation. Every recipe is a little different. In India vegetables are cooked for longer than in the West so that the spices will penetrate.

1 small cauliflower (400 g), trimmed
1 tbs sunflower seed oil
1 tsp whole cumin seeds
6 whole black peppercorns
350 g potatoes, peeled and diced
1 tsp each of turmeric, ground cumin and ground coriander
½ tsp chilli powder (optional)
200 g plain yoghurt

kitchen knife
tablespoon
teaspoon
wooden spoon
heavy based pan with a lid
basin

1 Cut the cauliflower into bite-sized pieces.
2 Heat the oil in a heavy based pan and fry the whole spices for about a minute until they begin to jump in the pan.
3 Add the cauliflower and potatoes and stir so that the spices are well distributed.
4 Mix the ground spices with the yoghurt and pour over the vegetables. Stir well.
5 Bring the mixture to the boil. Stir and cover with a lid. Reduce the heat and simmer for 40 minutes stirring from time to time.

Serves 4.   *Cooking time: 40 minutes.*

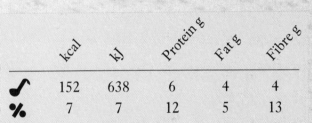

	kcal	kJ	Protein g	Fat g	Fibre g
🥄	152	638	6	4	4
%	7	7	12	5	13

Good source of vitamin C

◆ CHOW MEIN ◆

Unlike Chop Suey which was invented by Chinese navvies working on the American railways, Chow Mein is a traditional Chinese dish. Use any vegetables in season to enhance the taste or appearance of the dish.

1 clove garlic, finely chopped
2 tsp freshly grated root ginger
½ bunch spring onions, finely chopped
225 g lean pork meat, cut into long thin strips
4 sticks celery, thinly sliced
½ red pepper and ½ green pepper, seeded and cut into thin strips or any colourful vegetable in season
225 g Chinese dried egg noodles
2 tbs polyunsaturated cooking oil
2 tbs soy sauce
2 tbs water
salt and pepper
100 g beansprouts
½ bunch spring onions for spring onion flowers

kitchen knife   large saucepan
wooden spoon   large frying pan or wok
teaspoon   measuring jug (optional)

1 Prepare all the vegetables and the pork before starting.
2 Fill a large pan with water and bring to the boil. Plunge the dried noodles into it and leave for as long as directed on the pack.
3 Heat the oil in a large deep sided frying pan or wok. Add the garlic, ginger and chopped spring onions. Stir fry for 1 minute. Add the pork and continue to stir fry for 2–3 minutes until there is no pinkness showing when a strip of pork is cut in half. Remove the pork from the pan and keep on one side.
4 Add the celery and pepper or other vegetable strips to the remaining oil and stir fry for 2 minutes.
5 Return the pork to the pan and add the soy sauce, water and seasoning and bring to the boil. Cover and leave for 2 minutes.
6 Stir in the beansprouts.
7 Drain the noodles and serve with the pork and vegetable mixture on top. Garnish with spring onion flowers.

NB If more sauce is wanted with the pork add 100 ml chicken stock mixed with 1 teaspoon cornflour in place of the water.

Serves 4.   *Cooking time: 6 minutes.*

	kcal	kJ	Protein g	Fat g	Fibre g
♪	461	1924	25	19	5
%	21	21	46	23	18

◆ DEVILLED KIDNEYS WITH MUSHROOMS ■

The mushrooms have a similar texture to the kidneys in this recipe and help to make the helpings look more generous. Serve with brown rice.

8 lamb's kidneys
1 small onion, finely chopped
1 tbs polyunsaturated cooking oil
200 g button mushrooms, cut in half or quartered
1 tbs flour
4–6 tbs water
1 tsp Worcestershire sauce
1 tsp dry mustard
salt and pepper

kitchen knife
tablespoon
teaspoon

wooden spoon
saucepan
chopping board

1 Skin the kidneys, cut in half and remove the central core. Chop into chunks.
2 Fry the onion in the oil for 1–2 minutes and stir in the kidneys and mushrooms. Continue cooking for a further 2–3 minutes, stirring all the time.
3 Add all the remaining ingredients and bring the mixture to the boil. Cover and simmer for 15–20 minutes until the kidneys are tender.

Serves 4.   *Cooking time: 20–25 minutes.*

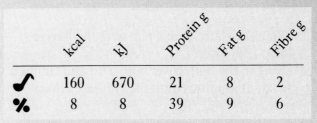

	kcal	kJ	Protein g	Fat g	Fibre g
🥄	160	670	21	8	2
%	8	8	39	9	6

Good source of iron

◆ RHUBARB FOOL

If you add a little lemon juice to rhubarb it helps to take away the very tart taste which sometimes makes your teeth feel 'furry'.

450 g rhubarb, trimmed and sliced
1 tbs lemon juice
1 tbs water
1–2 tbs sugar or honey
1 egg, separated
60 ml double cream, lightly whipped *or* yoghurt

kitchen knife   bowl
saucepan with lid   chopping board
tablespoon   sieve
whisk

1 Place the rhubarb in a pan with the lemon juice and water.
2 Bring to the boil, cover with a lid and simmer for 8–10 minutes until the rhubarb is very soft.
3 Rub through a sieve, or use a processor. Mix with the sugar and egg yolk and leave to cool.
4 Stir in the whipped cream or yoghurt.
5 Whisk the egg white until it is very stiff and fold into the rhubarb mixture.

Serves 4.   *Cooking time: 8–10 minutes.*

	kcal	kJ	Protein g	Fat g	Fibre g
✓	175	723	3	2	2
%	8	8	5	3	8

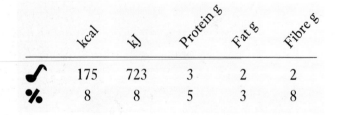

◆ RHUBARB AND GINGER CRUMBLE ◆

500 g rhubarb, trimmed and sliced
juice of ½ lemon
50 g raisins
4 tbs water
1 tsp ground ginger
Topping
75 g wholemeal flour
25 g medium oatmeal
50 g butter *or* hard margarine
25 g dark Muscovado *or* brown sugar

kitchen knife   lemon squeezer
tablespoon   1 litre ovenproof dish
teaspoon   mixing bowl

1 Set the oven to 190°C/375°F/Gas 5.
2 Place the fruit, lemon juice, raisins, ginger and water in an ovenproof dish.
3 Make the topping by placing the flour in a mixing bowl. Cut the fat into small pieces and rub in using the tips of the fingers. Stir in the oatmeal and sugar. Sprinkle over the top of the fruit.
4 Bake for 40 minutes. Serve hot or cold.

Serves 4.   *Cooking time: 40 minutes.*

	kcal	kJ	Protein g	Fat g	Fibre g
✓	240	1005	4	11	6
%	11	11	8	14	19

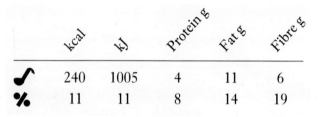

◆ CAULIFLOWER CHEESE ◆

For a more unusual flavour, cook a trimmed and halved head of fennel with the cauliflower.

1 cauliflower, washed and trimmed (500–600 g)
50 g butter
50 g wholemeal flour
milk
salt and pepper
100 g Edam cheese, grated
2 blocks shredded wheat, crushed

kitchen knife   small saucepan
wooden spoon   pie dish
saucepan   wire whisk
measuring jug

1 Place the cauliflower stem side down in a pan with 1 cm boiling water. Cover, reduce the heat and simmer for 10–15 minutes until the cauliflower is just tender.

2 Drain the cooked cauliflower retaining the cooking liquid. Make up to 450 ml with skimmed milk. Cut the cauliflower into florets and place in a heatproof pie dish. Keep warm.

3 Heat the butter, flour and milk in a pan whisking all the time with a wire whisk until it boils and thickens. Season to taste and cook for 2 minutes. Stir in 50 g cheese and pour the sauce over the cauliflower.

4 Mix the remaining cheese and crushed shredded wheat. Sprinkle over the top of the dish and brown under a hot grill.

Serves 4.   *Cooking time: 20 minutes.*

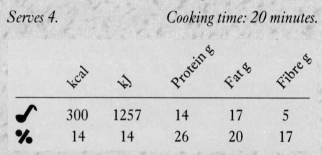

	kcal	kJ	Protein g	Fat g	Fibre g
🍴	300	1257	14	17	5
%	14	14	26	20	17

Good source of vitamin A and calcium

◆ STIR-FRY CHICKEN WITH BROCCOLI ■

Make sure that the fat in the pan or wok is really hot before adding the chicken or the vegetables. This gives the best results because the food is sealed immediately and does not soak up the fat.

3 chicken thighs, boned, or 2 small chicken breast fillets (approx 225 g)
2 tbs polyunsaturated cooking oil
1 clove garlic, finely chopped
2 tsp freshly grated root ginger
½ bunch spring onions, trimmed and sliced lengthways
225 g bunch broccoli cut into chunks
½ × 225 g can bamboo shoots, drained (optional)
1 tsp cornflour
2 tbs soy sauce
4 tbs water
freshly ground black pepper

kitchen knife
tablespoon
teaspoon
wooden spoon
deep sided frying pan or wok
chopping board

1 Skin the chicken and cut the meat into thin strips.
2 Pour the cooking oil into a deep sided frying pan or wok and place over a high heat.
3 Add the garlic and ginger and stir fry for 1 minute. Add the chicken pieces and stir fry for 2–3 minutes until there is no pink showing in the flesh when a piece is cut in half.
4 Remove the chicken from the pan or wok and keep on one side.
5 Add the spring onions, broccoli and bamboo shoots if using to the pan and stir fry for 2 minutes.
6 Mix the cornflour with the soy sauce, water and black pepper. Return the chicken to the pan and pour the soy sauce mixture over the top. Cover and cook for 2–3 minutes.
7 Serve with boiled rice and spring onion flowers.

Serves 4.   *Cooking time: 6–7 minutes.*

	kcal	kJ	Protein g	Fat g	Fibre g
🍗	230	958	12	18	2
%	11	11	23	21	8

Good source of vitamin C

◆ STUFFED LEAVES

Any kind of large green leaves can be used for this recipe. Choose from spring greens, hearted green cabbage, savoy cabbage, Chinese leaves or spinach. If you choose the latter pick out the largest leaves and use in twos.
NB The shredded wheat gives a softer texture to the filling while the cracked wheat is more grainy.

8 large leaves (16 for spinach)
300 ml tomato juice

Filling
50 g cracked wheat or 2 blocks shredded wheat
1 tbs sunflower seed oil
1 large onion
225 g minced beef
1 tbs tomato purée
3 tbs freshly chopped parsley
1 tbs freshly chopped mint or ½ tsp dried mint
pinch each of ground cinnamon and ground cumin
salt and freshly ground black pepper

kitchen knife   sieve
tablespoon   frying pan with lid
wooden spoon   kitchen paper
roasting tin   measuring jug
basin   chopping board

1 Place the leaves in a roasting tin and pour boiling water over them. Leave to stand while you make the filling.

2 Put the cracked or shredded wheat in a basin and cover with cold water. Leave to stand for 10 minutes. Drain very well in a sieve.
3 Heat the oil in a frying pan and fry the onion for 2 minutes. Add the minced beef and continue frying for 3–4 minutes. Drain off any excess fat.
4 Add the tomato purée, herbs, spices and seasoning and the drained wheat.
5 Drain the leaves and dry on kitchen paper. Place spoonfuls of the filling on each leaf and roll up into a parcel.
6 Clean the pan and place the stuffed leaves in it. Pour on the tomato juice and bring to the boil. Reduce the heat. Cover with a lid and simmer for 30 minutes.

Serves 4.   *Cooking time: 40 minutes.*

	kcal	kJ	Protein g	Fat g	Fibre g
♪	226	942	13	13	3
%	11	11	24	16	9

◆ BROCCOLI AND CHEESE FLAN ◆

Wholemeal pastry tends to be shorter and more crumbly than pastry made with white flour and it can be quite difficult to roll out. However, flan bases can be lined by rolling the pastry into a fairly thick round and placing this in the base of the flan tin. The pastry can then be worked up the sides of the tin with the fingers.

100 g wholemeal flour
½ tsp baking powder
pinch salt
25 g each white vegetable fat and hard vegetable margarine *or* 50 g hard vegetable margarine
25 g Cheddar cheese, grated
1 tbs cold water

Filling

175 g broccoli
1 small onion, peeled and sliced
salt
2 eggs, beaten
100 g low fat soft cheese, quark or fromage frais
75 ml skimmed milk
black pepper
25 g Cheddar cheese, grated

kitchen knife
teaspoon
tablespoon
fork
rolling pin
mixing bowl

20 cm loose based flan tin
small saucepan with lid
measuring jug
chopping board

1 Set the oven to 190°C/375°F/Gas 5.
2 Put the flour, baking powder and salt in a mixing bowl. Add the fat cut into small pieces. Using the tips of the fingers rub the fat into the flour until the mixture resembles fine breadcrumbs.
3 Stir in the cheese and add sufficient water to make a dough.
4 Roll out the pastry and use to line a 20 cm flan tin, working the pastry up the sides with the fingers if necessary.
5 Prick the base all over with a fork and bake in the oven for 10 minutes.
6 Meanwhile place the broccoli and onion in a saucepan with a little lightly salted boiling water. Cover with a lid and simmer for 10 minutes. Drain well.
7 Remove the flan from the oven. Cut the broccoli and onion into pieces and place in the base of the flan.
8 Beat the eggs with the soft cheese, milk and black pepper and pour over the top of the vegetables.
9 Sprinkle with grated cheese and bake for 40 minutes until set in the centre and golden in colour. Remove from the tin and serve or leave to cool.

Serves 4.   *Cooking time: 40 minutes.*

	kcal	kJ	Protein g	Fat g	Fibre g
♪	312	1305	17	18	5
%	15	15	32	22	15

Good source of vitamin A and calcium

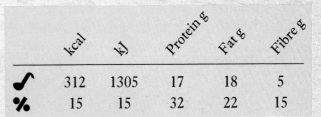

◆ PANCAKES WITH CHEESY SPINACH FILLING ◆

You can make pancakes with plain or with wholemeal flour. If using the latter you will find that you cannot make quite so many pancakes and they will be rather thicker than those made with ordinary flour.

Pancakes
100 g plain or wholemeal flour
pinch salt
1 egg, beaten
250 ml skimmed milk
cooking oil

Filling
450 g fresh spinach, washed
(*or* 200 g frozen spinach)
225 g cottage cheese
pinch nutmeg
salt and pepper

tablespoon   measuring jug
wooden spoon   heavy frying pan
sieve   kitchen paper
mixing bowl   fish slice

1 Sift the flour and salt into a bowl. Make a well in the centre and add the egg and half the milk.
2 Stir the mixture and gradually draw in the flour from the sides of the bowl. When all the flour has been mixed in, beat thoroughly with a wooden spoon and add the rest of the milk.
3 Heat a very little oil in a heavy frying pan. Stir the batter and put 2–3 tablespoons into the pan. Tip the pan so that the batter completely covers the base.
4 Cook for about a minute until the pancake is set and golden underneath and turn over. Cook the second side for another minute or so.
5 Continue until all the batter is used up wiping the pan each time with a wad of kitchen paper dipped in oil. Keep the pancakes warm.
6 Place the spinach in a large pan and cook over a medium heat for 2–3 minutes. Drain and dry on kitchen paper.
7 Return the spinach to the pan and add the cottage cheese, nutmeg and seasoning. Heat through over a medium heat. Place spoonfuls on the centre of each pancake and roll up.

Serves 4.   *Cooking time: 20–30 minutes.*

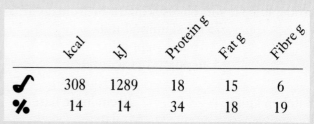

	kcal	kJ	Protein g	Fat g	Fibre g
♪	308	1289	18	15	6
%	14	14	34	18	19

Good source of vitamin A and calcium

◆ SPINACH AND TUNA ROULADE ◆

If the spinach is washed, drained and cooked at once there will be ample residual water in which to cook it. Adding more water will simply make it too wet.

450 g fresh spinach, washed
(*or* 200 g frozen spinach)
40 g butter
40 g 83% extraction flour
175 ml skimmed milk
salt and pepper
¼ tsp nutmeg
3 eggs, separated

Filling
1 × 200 g can tuna (canned in brine),
drained and mashed
150 g low fat soft cheese, quark or fromage frais

kitchen knife
wooden spoon   saucepan
teaspoon   sieve
Swiss roll tin (30 × 19 cm) wire rack
Bakewell paper   tea towel

1 Set the oven to 190°C/375°F/Gas 5.
2 Line a Swiss roll tin with non-stick paper.
3 Place the spinach in a pan, cover with a lid and cook over a medium heat for 3–4 minutes until the spinach is limp.

4 Drain very well, dry on kitchen paper and chop finely.
5 Heat butter, flour and milk in a pan. Bring to the boil, stirring all the time. The sauce should be quite thick.
6 Stir in the spinach, seasoning, nutmeg and egg yolks.
7 Whisk the egg whites until they are very stiff and add a tablespoonful to the spinach mixture. Fold in the rest of the whites.
8 Spread the mixture smoothly over the prepared Swiss roll tin and bake for 20 minutes.
9 Prepare the filling by mixing tuna with the soft cheese. Spoon into a pan and heat gently.
10 Cover a wire rack with a tea towel and turn the roulade on to this. Remove the paper and spread with the prepared filling.
11 Holding the tea towel in both hands gently roll up the roulade like a Swiss roll.

Serves 4.   *Cooking time: 25 minutes.*

	kcal	kJ	Protein g	Fat g	Fibre g
♪	294	1238	31	14	4
%	14	14	58	16	13

Good source of iron

FRUIT

What is a fruit?

People often muddle up fruits and vegetables. In science, a fruit is 'the ripened ovary of a plant containing the seeds'.

marrow   pumpkin   cucumber

Marrows, pumpkins, and cucumbers all contain **seeds**, so they are **fruits** not vegetables!

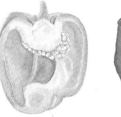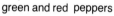

green and red peppers   aubergine   tomato

All these 'vegetables' are in fact **fruits**.

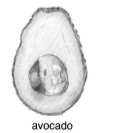

avocado   mango   plum

Some fruits such as avocados, plums, and mangoes contain large stones.

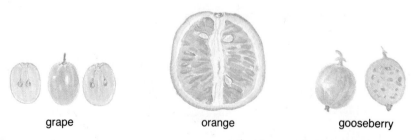

grape   orange   gooseberry

Some, such as grapes, oranges, and gooseberries contain many seeds.

Sort these foods into **fruits** or **vegetables**. Which ones are difficult to sort?
pears   cauliflower   okra   lettuce   rhubarb   raisins   tomatoes   runner beans

The food value of fruits

As fruits are mostly **water**, they contain few **kilocalories** and very little **protein**, **fat**, and **carbohydrate**. Fruits, like vegetables, are important in our diet since they contain **vitamin C** and **dietary fibre**. Vitamin C is needed to keep our bodies healthy and it helps absorb the iron from our food. Dietary fibre is the part of the plant which we cannot digest. Since fibre absorbs water, it increases the bulk of the food we eat and helps it pass easily along the digestive system.

Orange and yellow fruits such as mangoes and bananas contain **vitamin A**, which is needed to keep the skin and body tissues healthy and help our eyes adapt to dim light.

Fruit – save its vitamin C and dietary fibre!

1 Old and damaged fruit loses its vitamin C. So buy young fruit!

2 Fibre and other valuable nutrients are found in the skin, so avoid peeling fruits such as apples and pears.

3 Vitamin C is lost in cooking water and destroyed by heat, so stew fruit in a little water for a short time and try to use the water too.

4 When fruit is chopped up, vitamin C is lost, so prepare fruit only when you need it.

Work out the food value for each of these fruits. First you need to know how much they might weigh.
a) an apple   b) an orange
c) some grapes (a small handful)
d) a tomato

Vitamin C

Source: Bender and Bender

This picture shows the amount of vitamin C (in mg per 100 g) for each of the fruits and vegetables. But what does 100 g of each of these foods really look like? Find out!

1 Choose four of these fruits and vegetables and weigh out 100 g of each. Write down the name of the food and what 100 g actually looks like (e.g. three-quarters of a peeled medium-size orange).

2 How much of these four foods would you normally eat? An adult needs 30 mg of vitamin C a day: would these foods supply you with useful amounts of vitamin C?

How can fruit lose its fibre?

You need:

an orange	sharp knife
lemon squeezer	chopping board
	glass

1 Cut the orange in half. Draw this 'cross section' to show the pithy walls of the orange which hold the juicy fruit.
2 Squeeze the juice into a glass. Draw the squeezed half of orange.

Orange segments contain 1.5 g of fibre per 100 g. Orange juice contains no fibre.

Using your drawings of the squeezed orange, explain why orange juice contains no fibre.

What makes chopped fruit and vegetables change colour?

When fruit and vegetables are cut up, they begin to change colour. Cutting breaks down the cell walls of the fruits and releases the **enzymes**. These can react with air to cause colour changes and make the fruit decay.

Can you stop fruit changing colour?

Work in pairs or groups and choose a fruit or vegetable to investigate.

You need:

4 saucers or small plates	1 teaspoon of lemon
knife	juice
chopping board	salty water – a little salt
fruit or vegetable of your	in water
choice: banana, apple,	watch or clock
pear, potato . . .	

1 Label the saucers A,B,C,D.
2 Cut up the fruit into 4 equal slices and put a slice on each saucer.
3 Saucer A: leave the fruit uncovered.
   Saucer B: cover the fruit with a little water.
   Saucer C: cover the fruit with a teaspoon of lemon juice.
   Saucer D: cover the fruit with salty water.
4 Copy the chart and fill in your results. Keep a careful note of the time.

Fruit	Colour at start	change after 10 mins	20 mins	1 hour	later
BANANA					
Saucer A					
Saucer B					
Saucer C					
Saucer D					

1 Which fruits or vegetables in your investigation turned brown when cut?
2 Which other fruits and vegetables change colour when chopped up?
3 In your investigation which mixtures stopped the fruit from turning brown?
4 Why do you think in recipes: **a** lemon juice is used in fruit salad **b** sliced potatoes are sometimes left in salty water **c** lemon juice is sprinkled over avocado pear?

How much fruit do you eat and what does it cost?

As you prepare some of the recipes in the fruit section, weigh out the fruits that you use, and keep a note of how much they cost. Weigh out any parts that you could not eat – for example, peel, skin, and pips. Then weigh the *edible* fruit that is left, i.e. the fruit that you could eat. Copy and fill in the chart, using as many fruits and vegetables as possible.

How to work out the food value of fruit

	banana	orange	grapes
cost			
how much it weighs			
weight of peel, etc.			
weight of edible fruit			

Food tables give you the food value of 100 g of food. In real life, we eat different weights of food, so we need to know how much a banana or an orange weighs before we can work out its food value.

Copy this chart. The left-hand column shows the food value of 100 g of banana. In fact, you may eat 120 g of banana. Work out the food value of 120 g of banana and fill in the right-hand column.

kcal	80	kcal	96
kJ	330	kJ	
protein	1 g	protein	
fat	0.3 g	fat	
carbohydrate	20 g	carbohydrate	
water	70 g	water	
vitamin A	200 µg	vitamin A	
vitamin C	10 mg	vitamin C	
fibre	3 g	fibre	

How to work it out?

If there are 80 kcals in 100 g of banana, then how many kcals are in 120 g?
In 1 g of banana there are $80/100$ kcals = 0.8 kcals
So in 120 g banana there are 0.8 kcals × 120 = 96 kcals.

◆ FRESH FRUIT MILKSHAKE ■

Bananas, strawberries, and raspberries all make excellent milk shakes. Add more or less fruit to vary the strength.

150 ml skimmed milk
1 small banana, 3 or 4 large strawberries
or 1–2 tbs raspberries

food processor or blender

1 Place milk and fruit in the processor or blender and switch on at full power for about a minute.
2 Pour into a glass and serve at once.

Serves 1.

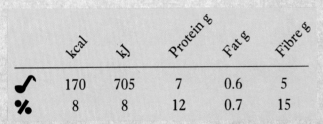

	kcal	kJ	Protein g	Fat g	Fibre g
🍴	170	705	7	0.6	5
%	8	8	12	0.7	15

Good source of calcium

◆ RAITA ■

In India yoghurt is used to make refreshing and cooling dishes which are served with hot curries. They may be flavoured with different fruit and vegetables such as potato, aubergine, cucumber, banana or walnuts. Serve with Aloo Gobi (see p.79) or Vegetable Curry (see p.101).

150 g carton plain yoghurt
3 cm piece cucumber, grated
1 tbs freshly chopped mint
½ tsp ground cumin
pinch cayenne or hot paprika pepper
salt and freshly ground black pepper

tablespoons   bowl *or* basin
teaspoon   grater
fork

1 Put the yoghurt in a bowl or basin and beat lightly with a fork until smooth and creamy.
2 Add all the other ingredients and mix together. Chill until required.
3 Serve sprinkled with a little more ground cumin.

Serves 2.

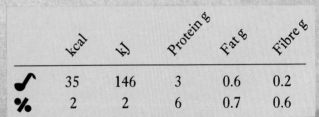

	kcal	kJ	Protein g	Fat g	Fibre g
🍴	35	146	3	0.6	0.2
%	2	2	6	0.7	0.6

Good source of calcium

◆ HIGH FIBRE BANANA BREAD ◼

This makes a very moist and fruity loaf.

30 g Allbran
100 ml skimmed milk
2 ripe bananas, mashed (approx 220 g)
50 g soft brown sugar
50 g raisins
225 g wholemeal flour
2 tsp baking powder
1 × 150 g carton natural plain yoghurt

teaspoon   basin
tablespoon   measuring jug
fork

1 Set the oven to 180°C/350°F/Gas 4 and grease and line a 450 g loaf tin.
2 Soak the Allbran in milk for 10 minutes.
3 Mix with the mashed bananas and stir in all the remaining ingredients.
4 Spoon into the prepared loaf tin and bake for 1 hour 20 minutes. Test with a skewer to see if it is cooked. Take out of the tin and leave to cool on a wire rack.
5 Turn out on to a cooling rack and leave to cool. *Makes 1 loaf (10 slices).*

Cooking time: 1 hour 20 minutes.

	kcal	kJ	Protein g	Fat g	Fibre g
🍴	139	587	5	0.7	4
%	7	7	9	0.8	13

Good source of iron

◆ FRUIT KEBABS ◆

Any kind of plentiful fruit in season can be added to these unusual kebabs.

	kcal	kJ	Protein g	Fat g	Fibre g
🍴	65	274	0.9	0.2	3
%	3	3	1.6	0.2	10

Basic fruit
1 small banana, peeled and cut into chunks (approx 100 g)
1 medium-sized red-skinned apple, cored and cut into wedges (approx 100 g)
1 tbs lemon juice

Seasonal fruit
Choose one or more of these fruits:
3–4 strawberries
2 apricots, halved and stoned
1 tangerine *or* satsuma, peeled and segmented
1 kiwi fruit, peeled and cut into wedges

kitchen knife   cocktail sticks *or*
chopping board   wooden skewers

1 Dip the chunks of banana and apple in the lemon juice to prevent them discolouring.
2 Thread the fruit onto skewers arranging them so that the different colours make an attractive pattern.

Serves 2.
Cooking time: Nil.

SKINNING AND PEELING FRUIT

It is much easier to skin fruit like tomatoes and peel citrus fruit like oranges and grapefruit if they are first plunged into a pan of boiling water. Leave in the pan for ½ minute and turn with a spoon to ensure that all parts of the fruit have been in the water. Remove from the pan with a slatted spoon and leave to cool for a minute or two before peeling.

◆ AVOCADO AND GRAPEFRUIT SALAD

The mixture of fruits in this tangy salad gives it a really interesting texture. Serve as a starter for four people or as a main lunch or supper dish for two.

1 grapefruit, peeled and
segmented (approx 200 g)
1 medium-sized avocado, halved, peeled
and stoned (approx 150 g)
½ green eating apple, cored (approx 50 g)
2 level tbs plain yoghurt
salt and pepper
4–6 lettuce leaves
sprigs of mint, basil *or* chervil

| kitchen knife | mixing bowl |
| tablespoon | chopping board |

1 Remove any tough membranes from the grapefruit and chop up the flesh. Place in a bowl with any juice which comes out.
2 Cut the avocado flesh and the apple into small chunks and add to the grapefruit with the yoghurt and seasoning. Toss well together.
3 Tear the lettuce leaves into smaller pieces and use to line the serving plates. Spoon the salad over the top.

Serves 4.

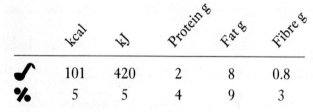

	kcal	kJ	Protein g	Fat g	Fibre g
🥄	101	420	2	8	0.8
%	5	5	4	9	3

Good source of vitamin C

◆ DRIED FRUIT SALAD IN ORANGE JUICE ◆

Dried fruits mix very well with fresh fruit but they need to be cooked first.

750 ml water
75 g raisins
100 g no-soak prunes
1 stick cinnamon
3 whole cloves
1 large pear, peeled and cored
2 clementines *or* seedless tangerines,
peeled and segmented
150 ml unsweetened orange juice

| kitchen knife | small saucepan with lid |
| measuring jug | chopping board |

1 Place the water, raisins, prunes and spices in a pan. Bring to the boil, cover and simmer for 10 minutes.
2 Cut the pear into chunks and add to the pan. Continue cooking for a further 10 minutes.
3 Remove from the heat and stir in the clementine or tangerine segments.
4 Leave to cool.
5 Stir in the orange juice and serve.

Serves 4.   *Cooking time: 20 minutes.*

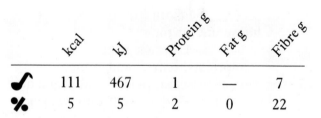

	kcal	kJ	Protein g	Fat g	Fibre g
🥄	111	467	1	—	7
%	5	5	2	0	22

Good source of vitamin C

◆ APPLE CRUNCH ◼

Choose any of the suggested ingredients for the crunchy layers and add to the chopped dried fruit, or add some more ideas of your own.

1 large cooking apple (approx 350 g), peeled, cored and sliced
2 tbs water
1 × 150 g carton plain or fruit yoghurt of your choice

Crunchy layers
50 g chopped raisins or dates or dried figs or apricots
4 digestive biscuits, roughly chopped
or
4 tbs rice crispies
or
3 tbs chopped peanuts
or
4 tbs bran flakes

kitchen knife   2 tall glasses
tablespoon   chopping board
small saucepan with lid

1 Put the sliced apples in the saucepan with the water.
2 Bring to the boil, reduce the heat and simmer covered for 8–10 minutes, stirring occasionally until the apples have fallen into a mush. Leave to cool.
3 Spoon a layer of apple into the bottom of two tall glasses. Add a layer of yoghurt and then a layer of dried fruit mixed with your chosen crunchy ingredient. Repeat the three layers again.

Serves 2.   *Cooking time: 3–4 minutes.*

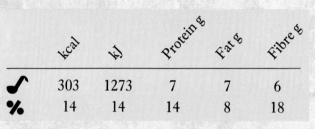

	kcal	kJ	Protein g	Fat g	Fibre g
🥄	303	1273	7	7	6
%	14	14	14	8	18

◆ PEARS IN ORANGE JELLY ■

Any kind of pure unsweetened fruit juice can be used in this recipe. For a change try bananas in apple juice or tropical fruit juice.

11 g packet gelatine
4 tbs water
500 ml pure unsweetened orange juice
2 large ripe pears, peeled, cored and sliced (400 g)

kitchen knife   measuring jug
tablespoon   4 ramekins
basin   chopping board
saucepan

1 Mix the water with the gelatine in a small basin and either:
   a) place in the microwave and heat for 1½–2 minutes on defrost. Stir to ensure gelatine is fully dissolved.
   b) Place the basin over a saucepan of boiling water and stir until the gelatine has dissolved.
2 Mix the dissolved gelatine with the orange juice.
3 Arrange the sliced pears in a glass dish or pie dish. Pour the orange jelly over the top.
4 Place in the fridge to set.

Serves 4.

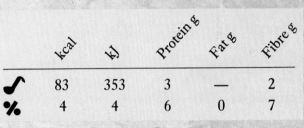

	kcal	kJ	Protein g	Fat g	Fibre g
♪	83	353	3	—	2
%	4	4	6	0	7

Good source of vitamin C

◆ COURGETTE CAKE

This unusual American cake has little flecks of green in it from the courgette skins. Serve with butter or margarine.

200 g plain or wholemeal flour
3 tsp baking powder
1 tsp light muscovado sugar
25 g raisins or sultanas
100 g grated courgettes
grated rind of 1 orange
1 egg, beaten
25 g margarine, melted
3 tbs milk

teaspoon
dessertspoon
grater
sieve
mixing bowl

loaf tin
greasproof paper
measuring jug
cooling rack

1 Set the oven to 190°C/375°F/Gas 5 and line the loaf tin with oiled greaseproof paper.
2 Sift the flour and baking powder into a bowl and stir in the sugar, raisins and the grated courgette and orange rind.
3 Add the liquid ingredients and mix to a soft dough.
4 Spoon into the prepared loaf tin and bake for 40 minutes.
5 Turn out onto a cooling rack and leave to cool.

Makes 1 loaf (10 slices).   Cooking time: 40 minutes.

	kcal	kJ	Protein g	Fat g	Fibre g
♪	105	441	4	3	2
%	5	5	7	4	7

◆ VEGETABLE CURRY ◼

Frying whole spices in cooking oil makes them more fragrant but less pungent and you will not need to worry about biting into them if they are fried for long enough.

3 tbs polyunsaturated cooking oil
½ tsp each whole cumin and coriander seeds and whole black peppercorns
2 whole cloves
3 tsp grated root ginger
2 cloves garlic, crushed
1 large onion, peeled and sliced (250 g)
150 g carrot, peeled and sliced
1 green pepper, seeded and sliced (100 g)
1 cooking apple, peeled, cored and sliced (200 g)
25 g raisins
150 g whole okra *or* sliced runner beans
2 tsp mild curry powder or garam masala
50 ml water
50 g frozen peas

kitchen knife
tablespoons
teaspoons

saucepan with lid
chopping board

1 Heat the cooking oil in a large saucepan. Add the whole spices and cook for 1 minute until they make a popping noise. Next add the ginger and garlic and fry for a further minute.
2 Stir in the onion, carrot and green pepper and continue to fry for 3–4 minutes.
3 Add all the remaining ingredients except the peas and bring to the boil. Cover and simmer for 30 minutes until the vegetables are cooked through and most of the liquid has been absorbed.
4 Add the peas and continue cooking for a further 6–8 minutes.

Serve with Raita (see page 93).

Serves 4.   *Cooking time: 45 minutes.*

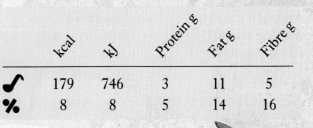

	kcal	kJ	Protein g	Fat g	Fibre g
🥄	179	746	3	11	5
%	8	8	5	14	16

◆ MALAY-STYLE CHICKEN

Coconut is used to flavour a great many dishes in South East Asia and other fruits are often included in savoury dishes. Use fresh or canned fruit depending on the time of the year. Use the juice from canned fruit to make fruit drinks with soda and lemon juice.

1 tbs polyunsaturated cooking oil
1 tsp each: ground cumin, coriander, turmeric
1 large onion (250 g), peeled and sliced
1 green *or* red pepper, seeded
and chopped (100 g)
¼ clove garlic, chopped
450 g chicken meat
50 g creamed coconut
250 ml stock
250 g freshly chopped pineapple flesh *or*
drained and chopped canned pineapple

kitchen knife
teaspoon
wooden spoon
chopping board

heavy based pan
with lid
measuring jug

1 Heat the cooking oil in a heavy based pan and fry the spices for ½ minute. Add the onion, pepper, garlic and chicken and fry for a further 2–3 minutes until the chicken is well sealed.
2 Next add all the remaining ingredients and bring to the boil. Simmer uncovered for 20–30 minutes until the chicken is cooked through. Larger pieces of chicken will take longer to cook.

Serves 4.   *Cooking time: 30–35 minutes.*

	kcal	kJ	Protein g	Fat g	Fibre g
🎵	222	924	25	8	2
%	10	10	46	8	5

◆ THAI PORK WITH ORANGE ■

Serve on a bed of crisp lettuce shredded with chicory or watercress.

1 large sweet orange, peeled (200 g)
350 g lean pork steak
½–1 clove garlic to taste
1 tbs polyunsaturated cooking oil
1 tbs finely chopped peanuts (25 g)
1 tbs soy sauce
a little grated orange rind
salt and pepper
¼ tsp mild paprika pepper

kitchen knife   chopping board
large frying pan   wooden spoon

1 Segment the orange retaining all the juice. Remove any pith or tough membranes. Cut each segment into 2 pieces.

2 Cut the pork into thin strips, discarding any fat or gristle.
3 Gently fry the garlic in hot oil for 1 minute.
4 Add the pork strips and stir fry until lightly coloured all over. Stir in the peanuts and continue to stir fry for a further minute.
5 Add all the remaining ingredients and the orange segments and juice and toss over a high heat. Serve on a bed of salad and pour any pan juices over the top. Garnish with spring onion flowers.

Serves 4.   *Cooking time: 5–6 minutes.*

	kcal	kJ	Protein g	Fat g	Fibre g
🍴	375	1573	16	33	1.5
%	17	17	30	40	5

Good source of vitamin C

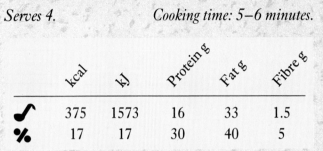

◆ VEGETARIAN MOUSSAKA ◆

If aubergines are not available or are particularly expensive use a larger quantity of potatoes. Salting the aubergines helps to drain off the bitter juices and also stops them taking up so much oil on frying. However, if time is short this step can be left out.

1 large aubergine (approx 450 g) with
stalk removed, sliced
salt
4 tbs olive *or* polyunsaturated vegetable oil
1 large onion (approx 450 g), peeled and sliced
225 g courgettes, diced
½ small green pepper (approx 50 g) seeded
and diced
1 × 397 g can tomatoes
1 tsp dried oregano
500 g potatoes
25 g margarine
25 g plain flour
300 ml skimmed milk
1 egg

kitchen knife   kitchen paper
tablespoon   two saucepans
teaspoon   measuring jug
wooden spoon   deep ovenproof dish
colander   chopping board
frying pan

1 Put the sliced aubergine in a colander, sprinkle with salt and leave for 20 minutes. Wash under the cold water tap and pat dry with kitchen paper.
2 Heat 3 tablespoons of the oil in a frying pan and fry the slices of aubergine until pale brown. Drain with a slotted spoon and dry again on kitchen paper.
3 Heat the remaining tablespoon of oil in the pan and fry the onion, courgette and green pepper for 2–3 minutes to soften and lightly brown them.
4 Stir in all the remaining ingredients and bring to the boil. Reduce the heat and simmer uncovered for 20 minutes, until soft and thickened.

5 Put the potatoes in a pan of boiling water and cook for 20 minutes. Peel and slice and keep on one side.
6 Make the egg sauce. Heat the margarine, milk and flour in a small pan, stirring all the time. As it boils, the sauce thickens. Remove from the heat and beat in the egg. Season with salt and pepper.
7 Set the oven to 190°C/375°F/Gas 5.
8 Prepare the moussaka by layering the aubergines, tomato and vegetable sauce and potatoes in an ovenproof dish. Spoon the egg sauce over the top and bake for 40–45 minutes until golden brown.

Serves 4. *Cooking time: 1 hour.*

	kcal	kJ	Protein g	Fat g	Fibre g
🥄	422	1767	11	22	8
%	20	20	21	26	27

◆ ITALIAN-STYLE LIVER WITH ONIONS

For the best results the liver should be sliced as thinly as possible. Take care not to overcook or it will go hard and leathery.

1 tbs olive oil
1 knob of butter (10 g)
575 g onions, peeled and sliced (500 g)
½ tsp dried thyme or sage
a little grated orange rind
juice of 1 orange
salt and pepper
350 g lamb's liver, thinly sliced

kitchen knife
teaspoon
wooden spoon
lemon squeezer

frying pan with lid
small bowl
chopping board

1 Heat the oil and butter in a frying pan and fry the onions for 4–5 minutes to soften them.
2 Mix the herbs, orange rind and juice and seasoning and pour over the onions. Bring the mixture to the boil, reduce the heat and simmer.
3 Lay the slices of liver over the top of the onions. Cover and simmer for 5 minutes.
4 Turn the liver over and continue cooking for a further 3–4 minutes.
5 Serve the liver with the onions on the side and the cooking juices poured over the top.

Serves 4. *Cooking time: 13–14 minutes*

	kcal	kJ	Protein g	Fat g	Fibre g
🍳	224	932	19	12	1
%	11	11	36	14	5

Good source of iron and vitamin A

SWEET APRICOT QUICHE

Use a mixture of wholemeal and plain flour to make a good sweet pastry. This unusual quiche may be eaten hot or cold.

Pastry
50 g wholemeal flour
75 g plain white flour
50 g margarine or butter
50 g sugar
2 tbs water

Filling
350 g can apricot halves, drained (210 g drained weight)
125 g low fat soft cheese
75 ml single cream
2 small eggs, beaten (size 5)

wooden spoon
fork
mixing bowl
kitchen knife

20 cm loose-based flan tin or flan ring with baking tray
measuring jug

1 Set the oven to 200°C/400°F/Gas 6.
2 Put the flour into a bowl and add the margarine *or* butter cut into small pieces.
3 Using the tips of your fingers rub the fat into the flour until the mixture resembles fine breadcrumbs. Stir in the sugar.
4 Add 2 tablespoons water and mix to a firm dough.
5 Roll out the dough and use to line a 20 cm loosebased flan tin.
6 Dry the apricot halves and arrange in the base of the flan.
7 Beat together the soft cheese, cream and eggs and pour over the fruit.
8 Bake in the centre of the oven for 40 minutes until the quiche is set in the centre and lightly browned on top.

Serves 6.   *Cooking time: 40 minutes.*

	kcal	kJ	Protein g	Fat g	Fibre g
🥄	274	1153	53	13	2
%	13	13	17	15	6

RASPBERRY AND MANDARIN FLAN

This sponge base is best filled just before it is to be served, otherwise it will go soggy.

2 eggs
50 g caster sugar
50 g self raising flour
200 g low fat soft cheese such as
quark or fromage frais
1 tbs sugar
a few drops vanilla essence
100 g fresh *or* frozen *or* canned and
drained raspberries
1 mandarin orange, peeled and segmented

bowl
wire whisk

tablespoon
18 cm sponge flan tin

1 Set the oven to 200°C/400°F/Gas 6 and grease a sponge flan tin. Line the centre base with greased baking paper.

2 Whisk the eggs and sugar until they form a thick foam and leave a trail.
3 Fold the flour in gently, using a tablespoon.
4 Spoon the mixture into the prepared flan and level off.
5 Bake for 10–15 minutes until it springs back to the touch. Leave to cool in the tin.
6 Mix the soft cheese with the sugar and vanilla essence and spoon into the flan.
7 Top with raspberries and mandarin segments.

Serves 6.   *Cooking time: 10–15 minutes.*

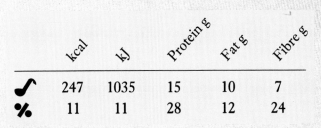

	kcal	kJ	Protein g	Fat g	Fibre g
♪	247	1035	15	10	7
%	11	11	28	12	24

Good source of vitamin C

◆ STUFFED MARROW ◆

If you want the marrow to be a little softer, peel before cooking.

1 small to medium sized marrow (approx 1.5 kg and 950 g after removing seeds)

Filling
300 g low fat sausages *or* sausagemeat
75 g wholemeal breadcrumbs
100 g mushrooms, finely chopped
1 tbs tomato puree
1 small onion *or* half a larger one, grated (100 g)
salt and pepper
pinch dried thyme

kitchen knife   mixing bowl
tablespoon   chopping board
fork   baking tray

1 Set the oven to 200°C/400°F/Gas 6.
2 Cut off each end of the marrow and then cut into four thick slices. Cut the seeds out of the centre and place on a baking tray.
3 Squeeze the meat out of the sausages and mix with all the other filling ingredients.
4 Spoon the mixture into the centre of each marrow ring.
5 Bake in the oven for 1 hour.

Serves 4.   *Cooking time: 1 hour.*

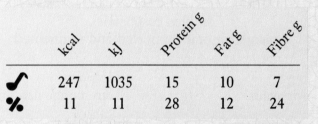

	kcal	kJ	Protein g	Fat g	Fibre g
♩	247	1035	15	10	7
%	11	11	28	12	24

SUGGESTED MENUS

Recipes from the book have been chosen and served with other foods to make a meal.

Breakfast	Muesli with milk Orange juice Soda bread with low fat spread, and marmalade
Lunch 1	Speedy sausage pizza Winter salad Baked apples with crunchy filling
Lunch 2	Chicken burgers Potato cakes Nutty adventure salad Rhubarb fool
Teatime snacks	Oatmeal scones, low fat spread, jam Courgette loaf with low fat spread
Supper 1	Leek and potato soup Wholemeal rolls Stir fried chicken with broccoli served with rice Pears in orange jelly, served with yoghurt
Supper 2	Chilli bean dip with fresh, crunchy vegetables Meat loaf served with jacket baked potatoes and boiled carrots Raspberry and mandarin flan
Supper 3 *Vegetarian*	Aloo Gobi Vegetable curry with rice Raita Fresh fruit kebabs

INDEX OF RECIPES

pears in orange jelly 99
pancakes
  stuffed with spinach 88
parsnips
  four vegetable dish with
    ginger 28
  harlequin fish pie 32
  pie 30
pasta pomodoro 59
peanuts
  American peanut butter
    cookies 46
  apple crunch 98
  crunchy filling for apples 44
  sauce for chicken satay 47
  soy cookies 42
  white rice salad 57
  winter salad 76
pears
  dried fruit salad 96
  in orange jelly 99
peas
  harlequin fish pie 32
  soup 40
  vegetable curry 101
peppers
  chow mein 80
  four vegetable dish with
    ginger 28
  Malay style chicken 102
  vegetable curry 101
pickled red cabbage 78
pineapple
  Malay style chicken 102
pizza
  speedy sausage 66
pork
  chow mein 80
  Thai with oranges 103
potatoes
  all-change salad 22
  aloo gobi 79
  and celeriac quiche 30
  cakes 24
  fish burgers 25
  soufflé 23
prunes
  dried fruit salad 96

radish
  raw root salad 21

raisins
  and beetroot salad 22
  and rye tea bread 65
  apple and oatmeal crunch
    bars 66
  apple crunch 98
  dried fruit salad 96
  Finnish fruit plait 69
  hot cross buns 68
  white rice salad 57
  winter salad 76
  vegetable curry 101
raita 93
raspberries
  fresh fruit milkshake 93
  raspberry and mandarin
    flan 107
raw root salad 21
red cabbage
  pickled 78
red kidney beans
  Mexican taco shells 50
rhubarb
  and ginger crumble 82
  fool 82
rice
  brown rice salad 57
  brown rice kedgeree 60
  flapjack 62
  white rice salad 57
roulade
  spinach 89
runner beans
  vegetable curry 101
rye and raisin tea bread 65

sausages
  stuffed marrow 108
scones
  oatmeal 62
sesame
  fish fingers 48
soda bread 63
souffle potatoes 23
soy peanut cookies 42
speedy sausage pizza 66
spiced lentils 49
spinach
  and tuna roulade 89
  filling for pancakes 88
  salad with crunchy
    croutons 77
  stuffed leaves 86

spring onions
  chow mein 80
stir-fry chicken 85
strawberries
  fresh fruit milk shake 93
  fruit kebabs 95
  stuffed leaves 86
  stuffed marrow 108
  sweet apricot quiche 106
sweetcorn
  chowder 56
  harlequin fish pie 32

tangerines
  dried fruit salad 96
  fruit kebabs 95
Thai pork 103
tomatoes
  pasta pomodoro 59
tuna
  Italian bean salad 41
  Spinach roulade 89
turnips
  golden root bake 26
  raw root salad 21

vegetable curry 101
vegetarian moussaka 104

watercress soup 74
wheat
  courgette cake 100
  Finnish fruit plait 69
  ginger and carrot bread 28
  high fibre banana bread 94
  hot cross buns 68
  pasta pomodoro 59
  rhubarb and ginger
    crumble 82
  soda bread 63
  winter salad 76

yam
  fish burgers 25
yoghurt
  aloo gobi 79
  apple crunch 98
  baked apple with crunchy
    chocolate filling 44
  beetroot and raisin salad 22
  chilli bean dip 38
  potato and celeriac
    quiche 30
  raita 93

INDEX